KEPT PURE

in all ages

Recapturing the Authorised Version
and the Doctrine of Providential Preservation

Jeffrey Khoo

KEPT PURE IN ALL AGES

Recapturing the Authorised Version and the
Doctrine of Providential Preservation

by

Jeffrey Khoo, PhD
Principal, Far Eastern Bible College

Far Eastern Bible College Press
Singapore

Kept Pure in All Ages: Recapturing the Authorised Version and the Doctrine of Providential Preservation

© 2001, 2021 (2nd edition) by Jeffrey Khoo
Published by Far Eastern Bible College Press (www.febc.edu.sg)
Printed in USA by The Old Paths Publications

Address all inquiries to:

THE OLD PATHS PUBLICATIONS, Inc.
142 Gold Flume Way
Cleveland, Georgia, USA 30528

Web: www.theoldpathspublications.com
E-mail: TOP@theoldpathspublications.com

Cover design: Eric Lim
ISBN: 978-1-7356723-8-0

To

My Dear Wife

JEMIMA

CONTENTS

ILLUSTRATIONS

FOREWORD

This latest book by Dr Jeffrey Khoo is what the whole Church, particularly its leaders and Bible College teachers and students should read.

It is an alarm bell to awaken the majority of uninformed believers to Satan's wiles during the last century to undermine the King James Bible by the spawning of a hundred new versions, the chief of which is the NIV. All these new "perversions" and the NIV are based on the corrupt text of Westcott and Hort.

These two Greek scholars, however, are now discovered to be enemies of Christ. They denied every fundamental of the Faith, including the infallible and inerrant Word, the Virgin Birth of Christ, His Blood Atonement and Resurrection. They called the Genesis account of the Creation and Fall a myth. They were close friends of Darwin and Freud whom *The Straits Times* called a Fraud. They were secret worshippers of Mary. They started the Hermes Club in Cambridge which was known as a homosexual den. From here they branched off into a Ghost Club which is condemned in Deut 18.

"Who shall ascend into the hill of the LORD? or who shall stand in his holy place? He that hath clean hands, and a pure heart; who hath not lifted up his soul unto vanity, nor sworn deceitfully" (Ps 24:3, 4). With unclean hands and impure hearts, how could Westcott and Hort touch Sacred Scripture?

Westcott and Hort have scissored out of the Bible 9900 words by alteration, by deletion, by substitution. This is equivalent to tearing off eight chapters of the Bible. And the NIV has also taken out the passage of the woman taken in adultery (John 7:53–8:11), the last 12 verses of Mark, and the verse on the Holy Trinity (1 John 5:7) from the Bible, though cunningly putting them back in truncated form to beguile the faithful to buy their product.

May God use this book to lead those who are using the NIV to abandon it. May the KJB which is founded on the Preserved Received Text bless you as it has blessed multi-millions during the last 400 years.

Rev Dr Timothy Tow

Founding Pastor,
Life Bible-Presbyterian Church

Founding Principal,
Far Eastern Bible College

PREFACE

There is a battle to be fought today. It is a battle for the Bible. The battle in the last century concerned the doctrine of Bible inspiration. In this new century, the battle concerns the doctrine of Bible preservation. The doctrine of inspiration is meaningless without the doctrine of preservation. The same God who inspired His Word has promised to preserve His Word. The Westminster Confession affirms the twin doctrines of Bible inspiration and Bible preservation: "The Old Testament in Hebrew (which was the native language of the people of God of old), and the New Testament in Greek (which, at the time of the writing of it, was most generally known to the nations), *being immediately inspired by God, and, by his singular care and providence, kept pure in all ages,* are therefore authentical."

This book originated with lecture notes for an evening course on the "KJV-NIV Debate" that I taught at the Far Eastern Bible College in 1998. The course was in response to certain ministers who sought to displace the KJV in favour of the NIV in our Bible-Presbyterian churches. By the grace of God, Life Bible-Presbyterian Church—mother of all B-P churches in Singapore—has taken a strong unequivocal stand for the KJV against the many modern perversions of the Bible (see "A Doctrinal Positional Statement of Life B-P Church," in her golden anniversary magazine, *50 Years Building His Kingdom*).

I am indebted to the works on the same subject by Mr David Cloud, Dr E F Hills, Dr D A Waite, the Dean Burgon Society, and the Trinitarian Bible Society. I have quoted much from these Bible-believing and Bible-defending scholars and institutions. I wish also to thank Mr Michael Maynard for his exhaustive research on the Johannine Comma (1 John 5:7), and Dr S H Tow, Rev Charles Seet, and Dr Dell Johnson for their respective charts and diagrams which in no small way enhance the pedagogic value of this book.

Last but not least, I am grateful to Rev Dr Timothy Tow—my teacher—for his indomitable spirit in earnestly contending for the faith

(Jude 3). Without his faithful and careful guidance, I would have fallen into the trap of the broad way of many corrupted Bibles. I now walk in the narrow way of one Bible—the Traditional Hebrew and Greek Texts that underlie the Authorised Version—which God has inspired and preserved for His people. May the Spirit move you to walk in the same narrow way as well (Matt 7:13–14).

CHAPTER I

INTRODUCTION

A 21ˢᵗ Century Battle for the Bible

There is a new battle for the Bible today. It is the battle for the Authorised or King James Bible and its underlying Hebrew and Greek texts over against the many modern versions and their corrupted texts. This battle seeks to recapture for the Church the traditional text and the doctrine of Bible preservation.

The battle is essentially between two opposing camps: the exclusivists (one Bible) versus the inclusivists (many Bibles). The former believes the King James Version (KJV) to be the most faithful, accurate, and trustworthy Bible in the English language, and thus promotes its exclusive use. The latter believes that most, if not all, Bible versions are in one way or other acceptable despite inherent corruptions, and that the church can safely use any of them. Of course, in either camp there are different shades of views. But generally the battle lines have been drawn quite clearly; either one is for or against the exclusive use of the KJV.

Since the top-selling Bible versions are the KJV and NIV, the battle is primarily between these two. The inclusivists usually promote the NIV over against the KJV. This book will thus examine these two versions. Which Bible version should Bible-believing and Bible-defending Christians use? The KJV or the NIV?

Ruckman or Burgon?

First of all, I would like to identify the KJV position that the Far Eastern Bible College (FEBC) has adopted. There are basically two types of KJV-only groups: (1) the Ruckman group, and (2) the Burgon group.

Ruckman

Peter Ruckman is president of Pensacola Bible Institute (not to be confused with Pensacola Christian College). He holds to the view that the KJV is separately inspired of God, contains advanced revelation, and thus superior to the original Hebrew and Greek Scriptures. Others who hold to this view are Texe Marrs, and Samuel Gipp. This position is erroneous because inspiration in the light of 2 Tim 3:16, and 2 Pet 1:21 is applicable only to the original writers (Moses, Matthew, John et al), original writings (66 books of canonical Scripture), and original languages (Hebrew, Aramaic, and Greek). Most anti-KJV books use Ruckman as the locus of attack. There are many KJV advocates who have distanced themselves from Ruckman, but many a time they are unfairly lumped together with him by KJV opponents. If by "KJV-only," Ruckmanism is meant, then we are not "KJV-only." Instead of "KJV-only," I prefer the term "KJV-superiority." More on Ruckman can be found in David Cloud's booklet—*What About Ruckman?* (Oak Harbor: Way of Life Literature, 1995).

Burgon

The Dean Burgon group of KJV advocates hold to a KJV-superiority view. This position is generally represented by D A Waite, President of the Dean Burgon Society, in his book—*Defending the King James Bible: A Fourfold Superiority* (Collingswood: Bible For Today, 1996), and the literature of the Trinitarian Bible Society. Others who belong to this group are Edward F Hills, David Otis Fuller, Thomas Strouse, Dell Johnson, and David Cloud. FEBC holds to this KJV-superiority view which is best expressed under section II.A of the Articles of Faith of the Dean Burgon Society: (1) "We believe in the plenary, verbal, Divine inspiration of the sixty-six canonical books of the Old and the New Testaments (from Genesis to Revelation) in the original languages, and in their consequent infallibility and inerrancy in all matters on which they speak (2 Timothy 3:16–17; 2 Peter 1:21; 1 Thessalonians 2:13)." (2) "We believe that the Texts which are the closest to the original autographs of the Bible are the Traditional Masoretic Hebrew Text for the Old Testament, and the Traditional Greek Text for the New Testament underlying the King James Version (as found in 'The Greek Text Underlying The English

JOHN WILLIAM BURGON (1813–1888)

Professor of Divinity, Oxford University
Dean of Chichester

John William Burgon was a man of deep faith and strong conviction, with an intense love of the Word, and a fierce loyalty to God's Truth. Raised of God at a time of great *"falling away"* from the faith, Burgon devoted himself with singleness of mind to defend the inspired Word of God by study of ancient manuscripts, the source texts of Bible translations.

Travelling extensively, he visited libraries throughout Europe, including the Vatican, to examine and study all available NT MSS. By his vast knowledge of Greek, he was able to identify those preserved NT MSS originating from the Apostolic church, and handed down intact up to the time of the Reformation.

To this group of preserved MSS, Dean Burgon gave the name of "Traditional Text," which formed the basis of the KJV, and continued to be used in the Protestant Church for the next three hundred and fifty years. He also identified the Codex Vaticanus and Codex Sinaiticus to be among MSS the "most corrupt."

Authorized Version of 1611' as published by The Trinitarian Bible Society in 1976)."

"We believe that the King James Version (or Authorized Version) of the English Bible is a true, faithful, and accurate translation of these two providentially preserved Texts, which in our time has no equal among all of the other English Translations. The translators did such a fine job in their translation task that we can without apology hold up the Authorized Version of 1611 and say 'This is the Word of God!' while at the same time realizing that, in some verses, we must go back to the underlying original language Texts for complete clarity, and also compare Scripture with Scripture."

The FEBC position statement of 1997 states that the KJV alone should be used as the primary Scriptural text in the public reading, preaching, and teaching of the English Bible. It is also stated that any Bible version that is a product of the dynamic equivalence method of translation, and casts doubt and/or omits verses based on corrupted readings of the Alexandrian or Westcott-Hort Text is deemed unreliable and thereby unworthy of use.

CHAPTER II

THE INSPIRATION OF THE BIBLE

There are three views on inspiration:

Natural Inspiration

Natural inspiration says that the Bible is inspired literature in the same way the works of Shakespeare are "inspired." The Bible is like any ordinary book written by man, and subjected to humanistic methods of study, analysis or interpretation. John D Crossan of the so-called *Jesus Seminar* says the Bible is "a mixture of myth, propaganda, and social convention." To such, the Bible is seen as a glorified *Aesop's Fables*. This view is held by the liberals.

Partial Inspiration

Partial inspiration says that the Bible is inspired only when it touches on matters of faith and salvation, but in the areas of science, history or geography, it can make mistakes. This is the position adopted by schools such as Fuller Theological Seminary. David Hubbard—former president of Fuller—said, "Where inerrancy refers to what the Holy Spirit is saying to the churches through the biblical writers, we support its use. Where the focus switches to an undue emphasis on matters like chronological details, the precise sequence of events, and numerical allusions, we would consider the term misleading and inappropriate" ("What We Believe and Teach," Fuller Theological Seminary, 1983). This view is held by the neo-evangelicals.

Total Inspiration

Total inspiration believes the Bible in all its 66 books is the divinely inspired Word of God, absolutely without error in whole and in part. The Constitution of the Life Bible-Presbyterian Church states, "We believe in the divine, verbal and plenary inspiration of the Scriptures in the original languages, their consequent inerrancy and infallibility, and, as the Word of God, the Supreme and final authority in faith and life." This is the view of conservative evangelicals and fundamentalists.

Biblical Meaning of Inspiration

The words "given by inspiration of God" in 2 Tim 3:16 come from one Greek word *theopneustos* which literally means "God breathed." It is thus not "manspiration," but "Godspiration." God used human writers to pen His words. These men were specially chosen by God, and perfectly guided by the Spirit to put on paper the very words of God, and to do so without any error (2 Pet 1:21).

All who believe and defend the Bible believe in what is known as Verbal and Plenary Inspiration (VPI): (1) Verbal Inspiration means every word of the Bible is inspired (Matt 5:18). (2) Plenary Inspiration means the Bible as a whole is inspired (2 Tim 3:16). VPI is well expressed by Dean Burgon: "The Bible is none other than the voice of Him that sitteth upon the throne. Every book of it, every chapter of it, every verse of it, every word of it, every syllable of it, every letter of it, is the direct utterance of the Most High. The Bible is none other than the Word of God, not some part of it more, some part of it less, but all alike the utterance of Him that sitteth upon the throne, faultless, unerring, supreme."

Inspiration and Translation

Are Translations Inspired?

"Does God 'breathe out' the words in the Spanish translation? Does He 'breathe out' the words in the French, or Russian, or English, or Japanese, or Italian, or Chinese? *No, He does not.* Strictly speaking, the words of the translations are not 'breathed out' or 'inspired,' but 'translated' words. God spoke in Hebrew/Aramaic and Greek words. God 'breathed out' these Words in Hebrew/Aramaic and Greek. So, strictly speaking, the only Words that were 'breathed out' or 'inspired words' were the Hebrew/Aramaic and Greek Words God gave to the writers" (D A Waite, "The Meaning of Biblical Inspiration," pamphlet #2237T [Collingswood NJ: The Bible For Today, nd]).

Accuracy in Translations

"We have the Words of God in English, or in Spanish, or in Italian, or in Portuguese, or in Russian, etc. This is true only in accurate translations like the King James Bible in the English language.

"God gave us His Words by a process of inspiration which will never again be repeated. God wants His Inspired Words of Hebrew/ Aramaic and Greek to be accurately translated into all the languages of the world (Rom 16:26, Acts 2:11). God expects us to find the most accurate Bible in our own language (In English, it is the King James Bible), and then read it, study it, preach from it, memorize it, live by it, and practice it the rest of our lives!" (Ibid).

One way of looking at the relationship between the original text and translation text of the Scriptures is that the former is a product of direct inspiration while the latter, if it is an accurate and faithful translation of the original, shares its inspiration only in the *derivative* sense.

For further study, read Edward F Hills, *Believing Bible Study* (Des Moines IA: The Christian Research Press, 1977), 1–53.

CHAPTER III

THE CANONICITY OF THE BIBLE

Meaning of Canon

The word "canon" literally means "a straight rod," or "a ruler." When applied to the Scriptures, it means the list of divinely inspired books—the Word of God—which serves as the only basis for faith and practice in the life of the Church.

Identification of the Canon

At Pentecost, God did not present the Bible to the Church as a complete whole. The canon of the OT was already confirmed (cf Luke 24:44, Luke 11:49–51), but not so for the NT. The books of the NT were written one at a time during the course of the first century. Shortly after that time, pseudo-books claiming inspiration were written. Which were the true divinely inspired canonical books? How was the canon arrived at?

The canon was arrived at by the ecclesiastical consensus of God's people who were indwelt and led by the Holy Spirit (John 16:13). The Council of Carthage (397), chaired by the pre-eminent early church father and theologian—Augustine—identified the sacred books by name. There were exactly 27 of them. The list presented was no innovation, but an official statement of what the Church had already accepted as canonical Scripture. It was a grassroots acceptance of the many churches that had been planted worldwide, and not just by a single church or denomination. It was by ecclesiastical consensus. The Westminster Confession states: "We may be moved and induced by the testimony of the Church to an high and reverent esteem of the Holy Scripture. And the heavenliness of the matter, the efficacy of the doctrine, the majesty of the style, the consent of all the parts, the scope of the whole (which is, to give all glory to God), the full discovery it makes of the only way of man's salvation, the many other incomparable excellencies, and the entire perfection thereof, are arguments whereby it doth abundantly evidence itself to be the Word of God: yet notwithstanding, our full persuasion and assurance of the infallible truth and divine authority thereof, is from the inward work of the Holy Spirit bearing witness by and with the Word in our hearts" (I.V).

Books of the Canon

The Canon thus consists of a total of 66 books as stated in the Westminster Confession: "Under the name of Holy Scripture, or the Word of God written, are now contained all the books of the Old and New Testaments, which are these

Of the Old Testament		
Genesis	2 Chronicles	Daniel
Exodus	Ezra	Hosea
Leviticus	Nehemiah	Joel
Numbers	Esther	Amos
Deuteronomy	Job	Obadiah
Joshua	Psalms	Jonah
Judges	Proverbs	Micah
Ruth	Ecclesiastes	Nahum
1 Samuel	Song of Solomon	Habakkuk
2 Samuel	Isaiah	Zephaniah
1 Kings	Jeremiah	Haggai
2 Kings	Lamentations	Zechariah
1 Chronicles	Ezekiel	Malachi

Of the New Testament		
Matthew	Ephesians	Hebrews
Mark	Philippians	James
Luke	Colossians	1 Peter
John	1 Thessalonians	2 Peter
Acts	2 Thessalonians	1 John
Romans	1 Timothy	2 John
1 Corinthians	2 Timothy	3 John
2 Corinthians	Titus	Jude
Galatians	Philemon	Revelation

All which are given by inspiration of God, to be the rule of faith and life" (I.II).

INSPIRATION

The New Testament autographs were written
by the Apostles under DIVINE INSPIRATION and
their texts have been PROVIDENTIALLY PRESERVED
through the ages.

PROVIDENCE

Trustworthy copies
were produced

Trustworthy copies
were read and copied

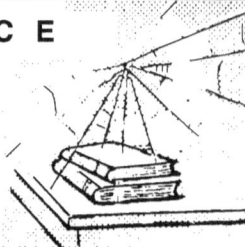

Untrustworthy copies
were not read or re-copied

RESULT

The original text has been faithfully restored

| God so loved the World | God so loved the World | God so loved the World | God so loved the World |

Words and phrases found in many manuscripts are trustworthy.
This is the leading principle of consistently
Christian New Testament Textual Criticism.

The difference between the Old and the New Testament text.
The Old Testament was preserved through the Aaronic Priesthood.
The New Testament has been preserved through the
Universal Priesthood of Believers.

(E F Hills, Believing Bible Study, 11.
Used by permission of The Christian Research Press, Des Moines, Iowa, USA.)

CHAPTER IV

THE TRANSMISSION OF THE BIBLE

We have today the 39 OT and 27 NT books. The Church accepts them as the inerrant and authoritative Word of God. The question is: Do we have the right text of those books since we do not have the autographs (i.e. the original books)? The answer is a definite yes.

Transmission of the OT

Method of OT Transmission

The OT was written over a period of 1500 years. The Lord used specially appointed people (e.g. Moses, David, Solomon, and the prophets) to write the OT Scriptures. The Lord by His Spirit inspired these men to pen His words infallibly and inerrantly. The OT was faithfully transmitted and preserved till the time of Jesus. Rom 3:1–2 tells us that to the Jews were entrusted the safekeeping and guarding of the Hebrew OT. Just how did the Jews safeguard the Scriptures to ensure that there would be no or minimal copying errors in the OT Scriptures? There were eight rules applied by the scribes in copying the Scriptures (H S Miller cited by D A Waite, *Defending the King James Bible*, 24–6):

(1) Preparation of a clean parchment taken only from the skin of clean animals.

(2) Each column consists of at least 48 lines, and contains no more than 60 lines. Lines must be drawn before any copying is done.

(3) The ink used must always be black, and is prepared according to a special recipe.

(4) The scribe is not allowed to write from memory. He must have an authentic copy before him. Before writing, he must first read and pronounce aloud each word. This is to prevent any duplications, or omissions of words.

(5) Whenever he has to write God's name (i.e. *Elohim*), he must first clean his pen. But before writing the name "Jehovah" (KJV "LORD"), he will have to wash his whole body. This is the kind of carefulness and reverence shown to God's Word.

(6) Strict rules govern the forms of the letters, spaces between letters, words, and sections, the use of the pen, and the colour of the parchment etc.

(7) If there is a need to correct the manuscript, it must be made within 30 days after the work is finished; otherwise the manuscript would be considered worthless. One mistake on a page condemned the whole page, and if there are three mistakes in any page, the entire manuscript is destroyed.

(8) The proofreading involves the laborious process of counting every word and every letter in the manuscript to ensure that it matches with the original. If there is an omission or addition of just one letter, or if one letter touched another, the manuscript was condemned and destroyed at once.

Significance of OT Transmission

Miller said that the above historic rules of OT transmission "show how sacred the Holy Word of the Old Testament was to its custodians, the Jews (Rom 3:2), and they give us strong encouragement to believe that we have the real Old Testament, the same one which our Lord had and which was originally given by inspiration of God" (Ibid, 26). Dr Robert Dick Wilson, co-defender of the faith with J Gresham Machen at Princeton Seminary in the 1920's, and proficient in over 40 languages, wrote: "In 144 cases of transliteration from Egyptian, Assyrian, Babylonian and Moabite into Hebrew and in 40 cases of the opposite, or 184 in all, the evidence shows that for 2300 to 3900 years the text of the proper names in the Hebrew Bible has been transmitted with the most minute accuracy. That the original scribes should have written them with such close conformity to correct philological principles is a wonderful proof of their thorough care and scholarship; further, that the Hebrew text should have been transmitted by copyists through so many centuries is a phenomenon unequaled in the history of literature. ... The proof that the copies of the original documents have been handed down with substantial correctness for more than 2,000 years cannot be denied" (*A Scientific Investigation of the Old Testament* [Chicago IL: Moody Press, 1959], 70–1).

Transmission of the NT

Periods of NT Transmission

The period of transmission covers 1400 years from the time of composition (1st century) to the invention of the printing machine (15th century). The history is divided into three periods: (1) Papyrus period (1st–4th century), (2) Uncial period (4th–9th century), and (3) Minuscule period (9th–15th century).

Papyrus Period

Papyrus manuscripts are continuing to come to light. A very important one just discovered is the papyrus—Magdalen GR 17—which will be discussed later. There are a total of 97 papyri according to the 4th edition of the UBSGNT.

Papyrus is found in Egypt, and is still being produced today, though more for tourists than for copyists. It comes from a large water plant by that name. The soft tissue-strips within the stem are used to make papyrus sheets. A papyrus sheet has two layers consisting of the horizontal and vertical strips. Writing is done on the smoother side where the grain is horizontal.

What is the length of a papyrus scroll? 2 and 3 John (13 and 14 verses respectively) would cover one column of one page of a papyrus (usually one page has two columns). Jude and Philemon would have taken two columns on a sheet. Revelation would have taken a scroll 15 feet long, Mark 19 feet, John 23 feet, Matthew 30 feet, Acts and Luke 32 feet. It is impossible on papyrus to have a complete scroll of the NT. It would take a 200 feet scroll to contain the whole NT. The papyrus scrolls were therefore circulated separately. This tells us three things: (1) the ignorance of a particular book does not mean it does not exist, (2) the scroll form makes it difficult to look up references, and (3) the scarcity of copies and difficulty in referring to specific passages, encouraged people to memorise the Scriptures.

Besides scroll-type papyrus manuscripts, there are also the codices. These are book-type papyrus manuscripts. The sheets are stacked together and sewn at the edge. This form existed from the third century onwards. Some suggest that Christians were the ones who invented the codex form. Obviously, this form allows for frequent reading and easier referring of the Scriptures.

Uncial Period

Uncial manuscripts are Greek manuscripts written in capital letters on vellum or parchment (i.e. leather usually calf-skin). There are about 300 extant uncial manuscripts; the more well-known ones are these:

(1) Codex Sinaiticus (ℵ) which was discovered by Tischendorf in St Catherine's monastery in 1844. There are four columns per page. Contains the complete NT and has much of the OT in Greek. Dated to about 350 AD (determined by the style of writing).

(2) Codex Alexandrinus (A) which is stored in the British Museum. Dated to about 400–450 AD. It is the longest and best known uncial manuscript. Contains the whole NT except for most of Matthew and some parts of John and 2 Corinthians. There are two columns per page. The gospels have the Byzantine text-type reading, while the others correspond to the Alexandrian text-type.

(3) Codex Vaticanus (B) which is kept in the Vatican library. It was found in 1481. Dated to about 350 AD. There are three columns per page. Contains both OT and NT, and Apocrypha. But almost the whole of Genesis, and the Pastoral Epistles, and Revelation are missing.

(4) Codex Ephraemi Rescriptus (C). "Rescriptus" means "to write again." Parchments were expensive, so people in those days recycled used parchments and wrote on top of the erased face. C was a biblical manuscript which had been erased, and Ephraem—a fourth century Church Father—wrote a sermon on the recycled parchment (or *palimpsest*). Contains parts of the NT except 2 Thessalonians and 2 John which are missing. Dated to about 450 AD.

(5) Codex Bezae (D) is kept in the Cambridge University Library. Dated to the sixth century. Contains the Gospels and Acts in Greek and Latin.

Minuscule Period

The minuscules appeared a little later than the uncials. A demand for books saw a change in writing styles. Minuscule or cursive writing was a lot faster than uncial writing. The letters are smaller, and in formal running hand. Over 90% of the 5,000 extant Greek texts are from Byzantine text-type. And out of a total of about 2,800 minuscules, 99% belong to the Byzantine text-type which underlies the KJV.

Types of Scribal Errors in NT Transmission

Since there were no printing or photocopying machines in those early days, the production of copies of the NT manuscripts was done painstakingly by hand, word for word. This tedious process would invariably result in some copying errors experienced even today by typists on electronic typewriters or computers. Many errors were accidental but there were those that were intentional.

The following lists the common types of copyist errors in the transmission of the Greek NT:

Errors of the Eye

Wrong Word Division

This can easily occur because some manuscripts do not leave spaces between words. How would you divide this string of letters? For example, HAVEYOUSEENABUNDANCE can be HAVE YOU SEEN ABUNDANCE, or HAVE YOU SEEN A BUN DANCE. Another example, GODISNOWHERE can be GOD IS NOWHERE or GOD IS NOW HERE.

Mistaking One Word for Another

This can happen especially when words are all in capital letters. E.g. Π and TI, M and ΛΛ.

Words with Similar Endings

This is an error when the scribe's eye skips over words or sentences to the next similar word or sentence. A mistake is made when a word that occurs once is copied twice, or a word that occurs twice but is written only once.

Errors of the Ear

This occurs during dictation. A wrong pronunciation of a word by the reader can lead to the writing of the wrong word by the copier.

Errors of the Mind

This occurs when the scribe, having memorised a portion of scripture, fails to remember accurately the verse or passage when putting it on paper.

Errors of Judgment

Words or notes written on the margin of an older manuscript were sometimes accidentally incorporated into the text of a new manuscript. Abbreviations can also be mistaken for something else. Eg: ΘΣ (GOD) and ΟΣ (HE WHO). It is likely that the change in 1 Tim 3:16 from "God" (TR/KJV) to "He" (WH/NIV) was an intentional one to obfuscate the deity of Christ.

By the providential hand of God, all such typographical and transmission errors, both accidental and intentional, have been corrected by 1611 in the Textus Receptus underlying the Authorised Version or KJV. The printing machine invented during the 15th century has removed the need to hand copy the Scriptures, thereby preventing any scribal errors from recurring in the transmission process.

CHAPTER V

THE PRESERVATION OF THE BIBLE

Preservation of the OT

We know that the OT was providentially preserved down through the ages because Jesus Himself said so. We can infer from Jesus' words in Matt 5:18 that every jot and tittle of the OT up till His time was faithfully transmitted and preserved without error. He considered the 39 OT books He had, comprising the Law, the Prophets, and the Writings, to be the inspired Word of God (Matt 4:4, Luke 24:27, 24:44).

Dr Hills wrote, "During His earthly life the Lord Jesus Christ appealed unreservedly to the very words of the Old Testament text (Matt 22:42–45; John 10:34–36), thus indicating His confidence that this text had been accurately transmitted. ... [In Matt 5:18, and Luke 16:17] our Lord assures us that the Old Testament text in common use among the Jews during His earthly ministry was an absolutely trustworthy reproduction of the original text written by Moses and the other inspired authors. Nothing had been lost from that text. ...

"Moreover, our Saviour's statements are also promises that the providential preservation of the Old Testament text shall never cease or fail. That same Old Testament text which was preserved in its purity during the Old Testament dispensation shall continue to be faithfully preserved during the New Testament dispensation until this present world is brought to an end ... The true Old Testament text shall be preserved in the Church *till all be fulfilled*. So our Lord has promised, and today the Holy Spirit gives to all true believers the assurance that their Saviour has kept and will keep His promise. As the believer reads the extant text of the Old Testament Scriptures, the Holy Spirit prepares his heart to receive its message with confidence and to recognize with gladness that the Old Testament as it exists today is a trustworthy reproduction of the Old Testament text that was first written down by

NEW TESTAMENT GREEK TEXT

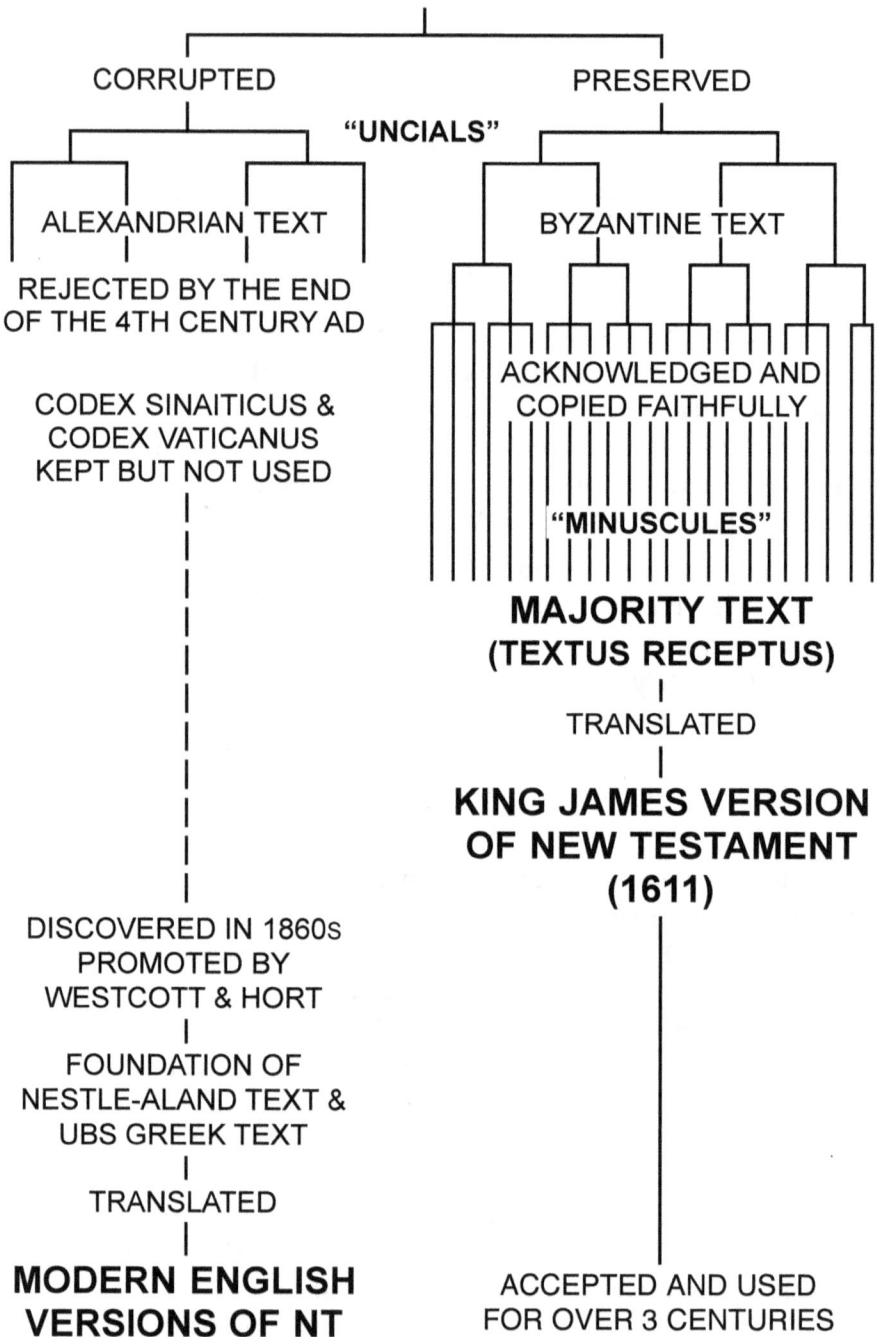

CORRUPTED

PRESERVED

"UNCIALS"

ALEXANDRIAN TEXT

REJECTED BY THE END
OF THE 4TH CENTURY AD

CODEX SINAITICUS &
CODEX VATICANUS
KEPT BUT NOT USED

BYZANTINE TEXT

ACKNOWLEDGED AND
COPIED FAITHFULLY

"MINUSCULES"

MAJORITY TEXT
(TEXTUS RECEPTUS)

TRANSLATED

KING JAMES VERSION
OF NEW TESTAMENT
(1611)

DISCOVERED IN 1860s
PROMOTED BY
WESTCOTT & HORT

FOUNDATION OF
NESTLE-ALAND TEXT &
UBS GREEK TEXT

TRANSLATED

MODERN ENGLISH
VERSIONS OF NT

ACCEPTED AND USED
FOR OVER 3 CENTURIES

inspired authors and then used by Jesus in the days of His earthly ministry" (*Believing Bible Study*, 6–7).

Dr Wilson the great OT scholar of Princeton said, "The results of those 30 years' study which I have given to the text has been this: I can affirm that there's not a page of the Old Testament in which we need have any doubt. We can be absolutely certain that substantially we have the text of the Old Testament that Christ and the Apostles had and which was in existence from the beginning" (*Which Bible?*, 1ˢᵗ ed, 80–1, cited by Waite, *Defending the King James Bible*, 35).

Preservation of the NT

Dean Burgon wrote of the preservation of the NT through the multitude of manuscript copies: "The provision, then which the Divine Author of Scripture is found to have made for the preservation of His written Word, is of a peculiarly varied and highly complex description, First—By causing that a vast multiplication of Copies should be required all down the ages,—beginning at the earliest period, and continuing in an ever-increasing ratio until the actual invention of Printing,—He provided the most effectual security imaginable against fraud. True, that millions of the copies so produced have long since perished; but it is nevertheless a plain fact that there survive of the Gospels alone upwards of one thousand copies in the present day" (*Revision Revised* [Collingswood NJ: Dean Burgon Society Press, nd], 8–9).

Textus Receptus and Providential Preservation

"The defense of the Textus Receptus, therefore, is a necessary part of the defense of Protestantism. It is entailed by the logic of faith, the basic steps of which are as follows:

(1) "First, the Old Testament text was preserved by the Old Testament priesthood and the scribes and scholars that grouped themselves around that priesthood (Deut. 31:24–26).

(2) "Second, the New Testament text has been preserved by the universal priesthood of believers, by faithful Christians in every walk of life (1 Peter 2:9).

(3) "Third, the Traditional Text, found in the vast majority of the Greek New Testament manuscripts, is the True Text because it represents the God-guided usage of this universal priesthood of believers.

(4) "Fourth, the first printed text of the Greek New Testament was not a blunder or a set-back but a forward step in the providential preservation of the New Testament. Hence the few significant departures of that text from the Traditional Text are only God's providential corrections of the Traditional Text in those few places in which such corrections were needed.

(5) "Fifth, through the usage of Bible-believing Protestants God placed the stamp of His approval on this printed text, and it became the Textus Receptus (Received Text)" (Hills, *King James Version Defended* [Des Moines IA: The Christian Research Press, 1984], 193).

Textus Receptus Editors and Providential Guidance

Dr Hills concluded, "Hence, as orthodox Protestant Christians, we believe that the formation of the Textus Receptus was guided by the special providence of God. There were three ways in which the editors of the Textus Receptus, Erasmus, Stephanas, Beza, and the Elzevirs, were providentially guided.

(1) "In the first place, they were guided by the manuscripts which God in His providence had made available to them.

(2) "In the second place, they were guided by the providential circumstances in which they found themselves.

(3) "Then in the third place, and most of all they were guided by the common faith. Long before the Protestant Reformation, the God-guided usage of the Church had produced throughout Western Christendom a *common faith* concerning the New Testament text, namely, a general belief that the currently received New Testament text, primarily the Greek text and secondarily the Latin text, was the True New Testament Text which had been preserved by God's special providence. It was this common faith that guided Erasmus and the other early editors of the Textus Receptus" (Ibid).

Psalm 12:6–7 on Bible Preservation

Ps 12:6–7 says, "The words of the LORD are pure words: as silver tried in a furnace of earth, purified seven times. Thou shalt <u>keep</u> them, O LORD, thou shalt <u>preserve</u> them from this generation for ever." What do the (1) "keep," and (2) "preserve" mean? (1) The Hebrew *shamar* means "to keep," "to guard," or "to observe." The basic idea is "to exercise great care over" (TWOT sv "שׁמר," by J E Hartley). It is used 461 times in the OT, and most of the time with reference to paying careful attention to the Word of God. In Ps 12:7, it has to do with the safeguarding of the purity of God's Word. God ensures the protection of His Word from perversion. (2) *Natsar*, a synonym for the above, means "to watch," "to guard," "to keep," "to preserve." It is used about 60 times in the OT, and when used in connection with God's Word, it has the concept of "guarding with fidelity" (TWOT, sv "נצר," by W C Kaiser). The faithfulness of God in guarding His Word from corruption is the intrinsic idea of the word here in Ps 12:7.

What does Ps 12:6–7 mean? D A Waite comments, "The word 'them' in verse seven refers back to 'the words of the LORD.' That is a promise of Bible preservation. God has promised to 'PRESERVE' His 'PURE WORDS.' This promise extends *from this generation* [that is, that of the Psalmist] *FOR EVER*." That is a long time, is it not? God is able to do this, and He has done it! He has kept His Words even more perfectly, if that is possible, than He keeps the stars in their course and the sun, moon, and all the other heavenly bodies in their proper place" (*Defending the King James Bible*, 6–7). An excellent defence of Ps 12 in support of Bible preservation is found in Shin Yeong Gil, "God's Promise to Preserve His Word: An Exegetical Study of Psalm 12:5–7," ThM thesis, Far Eastern Bible College, 1999, published in *The Burning Bush* 6 (2000): 150–182.

Other passages are Pss 33:11, 100:5, 111:7–8, 117:2, 119:89,152,160; Isa 40:8, 59:21 (John Owen called this verse "the great charter of the church's preservation of truth"); Matt 5:18, 24:35; 1 Pet 1:23,25; Rev 22:18–19.

Westminster Confession on Bible Preservation

The Westminster Confession states, "The Old Testament in Hebrew (which was the native language of the people of God of old), and the New Testament in Greek (which, at the time of the writing of it, was most generally known to the nations), being immediately inspired by God, *and by His singular care and providence, kept pure in all ages*, are therefore authentical; so as, in all controversies of religion, the Church is finally to appeal unto them" (I.VIII).

Dean Burgon Society on Bible Preservation

The Dean Burgon Society articles of faith reads, "We believe that the Texts which are closest to the original autographs of the Bible are the Traditional Masoretic Hebrew Text for the Old Testament, and the Traditional Greek Text for the New Testament underlying the King James Version (as found in *The Greek Text Underlying the English Authorized Version of 1611* as published by The Trinitarian Bible Society in 1976).

"We believe that the King James Version (or Authorized Version) of the English Bible is a true, faithful, accurate translation of these two *providentially preserved* Texts, which in our time has no equal among all of the other English Translations. The translators did such a fine job in their translation task that we can without apology hold up the Authorized Version of 1611 and say 'This is the Word of God!' while at the same time realizing that, in some verses, we must go back to the underlying original language Texts for complete clarity, and also compare Scripture with Scripture" (Articles of Faith, II.A).

Dr Edward F Hills on Bible Preservation

Dr Hills who has a ThD from Harvard affirmed the doctrine of biblical inspiration and preservation: "If the doctrine of *divine inspiration* of the Old and New Testament Scriptures is a true doctrine, the doctrine of the *providential preservation* of these Scriptures must also be a true doctrine. It must be that down through the centuries God has exercised a special, providential control over the copying of the Scriptures and the preservation and use of the original text have been available to God's people in every age. God must have done this, for if He gave the Scriptures to His Church by inspiration as the perfect and final revelation of his will, then it is obvious that He would not allow this revelation to disappear or undergo any alteration of its fundamental character.

"... if the doctrines of the *divine inspiration* and *providential preservation* of these Scriptures are true doctrines, then the textual criticism of the New Testament is different from that of the uninspired writings of antiquity. The textual criticism of any book must take into account the conditions under which the original manuscripts were written and also under which the copies of these manuscripts were made and preserved. But if the doctrines of the divine inspiration and providential preservation of the Scriptures are true, then **the original New Testament manuscripts were written under special conditions, under the inspiration of God, and the copies were made and preserved under special conditions, under the singular care and providence of God**" (*The King James Version Defended*, 2).

Against biblical scholars who reject the doctrine of providential preservation of Scripture, Hills wrote,

"If we ignore the providential preservation of the Scriptures and defend the New Testament text in the same way that we defend the texts of other ancient books, then we are following the logic of unbelief. For the special, providential preservation of the holy Scriptures is a *fact* and an important fact. Hence when we ignore this fact and deal with the text of the New Testament as we would with the text of other books, we are behaving as unbelievers behave. We are either denying that the providential preservation of the Scriptures is a fact, or else we are saying that it is not an important fact, not important enough to be considered when dealing with the New Testament text. But if the providential preservation of the Scriptures is not important, why is the infallible inspiration of the original Scriptures important? If God has not preserved the Scriptures by His special providence, why would He have infallibly inspired them in the first place? And if the Scriptures are not infallibly inspired, how do we know that the Gospel message is true? And if the Gospel message is not true, how do we know that Jesus is the Son of God?

"It is a dangerous error therefore to ignore the special, providential preservation of the holy Scriptures and to seek to defend the New Testament text in the same way in which we would defend the texts of other ancient books. For the logic of this unbelieving attitude is likely to lay hold upon us and cast us down into a bottomless pit of uncertainty. ...

"The Bible teaches us that faith is the foundation of reason. *Through faith we understand* (Heb. 11:3). By faith we lay hold on God as He reveals Himself in the holy Scriptures and make Him the starting point of all our thinking. ...

"Like the Protestant Reformers therefore we must take God as the starting point of all our thinking. We must *begin* with God. Very few Christians, however, do this consistently. For example, even when a group of conservative Christian scholars meet for the purpose of defending the Textus Receptus and the King James Version, you will find that some of them want to do this in a rationalistic, naturalistic way. Instead of beginning with God, they wish to begin with facts viewed apart from God, with details concerning the New Testament manuscripts which must be regarded as true (so they think) no matter whether God exists or not. ...

"Conservative scholars ... say that they believe in the special, providential preservation of the New Testament text. Most of them really don't though, because, as soon as they say this, they immediately reduce this special providential preservation to the vanishing point in order to make room for the naturalistic theories of Westcott and Hort. As we have seen, some say that the providential preservation of the New Testament means merely that the same "substance of doctrine" is found in all the New Testament documents. Others say that it means that the true reading is always present in at least one of the thousands of extant New Testament manuscripts. And still other scholars say that to them the special, providential preservation of the Scriptures means that the true New Testament text was providentially discovered in the mid-19th century by Tischendorf, Tregelles, and Westcott and Hort after having been lost for 1,500 years.

"If you adopt one of these false views of the providential preservation of Scriptures, then you are logically on your way toward the denial of the infallible inspiration of the Scriptures. For if God has preserved the Scriptures so carelessly, why would he have infallibly inspired them in the first place? It is not sufficient therefore merely to say that you believe in the doctrine of the special, providential preservation of holy Scriptures. You must *really* believe this doctrine and allow it to guide your thinking. You must begin with Christ and the Gospel and proceed according to the logic of faith. This will lead you to the Traditional text, the Textus Receptus, and the King James Version, in other words, to the common faith" (*Believing Bible Study*, 216–20).

Dr William Whitaker on Bible Preservation

Dr Whitaker who was Regius Professor of Divinity in the University of Cambridge in the 16th century likewise affirmed the doctrine of the providential preservation of Scripture: "If God had permitted the scripture to perish in the Hebrew and Greek originals, in which it was first published by men divinely inspired, he would not have provided sufficiently for his church and for our faith. From the prophetic and apostolic scripture the church takes its origin and the faith derives its source ... We must hold, therefore, that we have now those very ancient scriptures which Moses and the other prophets published, although we have not, perhaps, precisely the same forms and shapes of the letters" (Douglas W Taylor, "Pure Words, Preserved Words: The Doctrine of Providential Preservation," *Australian Beacon* [July 1995]: 3).

Dean J W Burgon on Bible Preservation

Dean Burgon of Oxford and Chichester rightly said, "If you and I believe that the original writings of the Scriptures were verbally inspired by God, then of necessity they must have been providentially preserved through the ages" (Jack Moorman, *Modern Bibles—the Dark Secret* [Los Osos CA: Fundamental Evangelistic Association, nd], 41).

Dr Timothy Tow on Bible Preservation

Dr Timothy Tow, principal of Far Eastern Bible College, likewise noted, "We believe the preservation of Holy Scripture and its Divine inspiration stand in the same position as providence and creation. If Deism teaches a Creator who goes to sleep after creating the world is absurd, to hold to the doctrine of inspiration without preservation is equally illogical. ... Without preservation, all the inspiration,

Godbreathing into the Scriptures, would be lost. But we have a Bible so pure and powerful in every word and it is so because God has preserved it down through the ages."

Bible inspiration and Bible preservation are twin doctrines. Like Siamese twins they are intrinsically linked, and cannot be separated.

For further study, read Edward F Hills, *The King James Version Defended*, 90–111; *Way of Life Encyclopedia of the Bible and Christianity*, sv "Preservation—Bible."

WILLIAM TYNDALE (1494–1536)

William Tyndale, master linguist of Oxford and Cambridge Universities, gave his people their first Bible translated from the original languages. By selfless toil, he completed translating the NT in 1525 and most of the OT before his death. Tyndale's Bible became a forerunner of the King James Bible (1611).

His testimony on translation,

> I call God to record against the day we shall appear before our Lord Jesus, to give a reckoning of our doings, that I never altered one syllable of God's Word against my conscience, nor would this day, if all that is in the earth, whether it be pleasure, honour, or riches, might be given me.

CHAPTER VI

THE TRANSLATION OF THE BIBLE

Westminster Confession on Translation

God originally gave the Old Testament in Hebrew/Aramaic, and the New Testament in Greek. "But because these original tongues are not known to all the people of God, who have right unto, and interest in the Scriptures, and are commanded, in the fear of God, to read and search them, therefore *they are to be translated into the vulgar (i.e. "common," or "vernacular") language of every nation unto which they come*, that, the Word of God dwelling plentifully in all, they may worship Him in an acceptable manner; and, through patience and comfort of Scriptures, may have hope" (I.VIII, parenthesis mine).

The Bible in World Languages

The Almanac of the Christian World (1991–2 ed) has the following Bible translation statistics: (1) Bible Portions: 899 languages, (2) Testaments: 715, and (3) Complete Bibles: 314. We thank the Lord for the translation of His Word into so many languages of the world. This is surely in partial fulfillment of Christ's Great Commission to His Church in Matt 28:18–20. However, the Church must be concerned not just in the *quantity* of translations but also in the *quality* of translation. The quality of translation has to do with translational methodology.

Methods of Translation

Formal Equivalence Method

This is the literal approach which translates the words of the original language into *the equivalent words* of the receptor language. It is a word-for-word translation. The Scripture itself employs this method of translation. Matt 1:23 translates the Hebrew *Immanu El* in Isa 7:14 as *Meth' hemon ho theos*, literally, "God with us." Another example is Matt 27:46, "*Eli, Eli, lama sabachthani;*" which is translated literally by Matthew as "My God, my God, why hast thou forsaken me?"

The formal equivalence method of translation is the only acceptable method for the translation of the Holy Scriptures because of the Scripture's verbally inspired nature. Since every word of the Bible is inspired of God, it goes without saying that a translation of His Word must be done as literally as possible, reproducing accurately in the receptor language what is written in the Hebrew, Aramaic, and Greek texts. The operating principle of this method of translation is: as literal as possible, as idiomatic as necessary. It is thus not an interlinear or woodenly literal approach. This philosophy of translation has been the standard for most Bible translators throughout the centuries. But today, we are introduced to a new approach called the dynamic equivalence method.

Dynamic Equivalence Method

G W and D E Anderson—editorial consultants of the Trinitarian Bible Society—commented, "In recent years, however, there has arisen a group of scholars who no longer believe in the importance, and often the inerrancy and inspiration, of the individual words of Scripture. These men believe instead that it is the thoughts or the truth behind the words that is important. ... This view is called the dynamic view of Scripture; transferred into the realm of translation, this is referred to as dynamic equivalence. The aim in dynamic equivalence translation is not word-for-word accuracy, but thought-for-thought equivalence."

The dynamic approach is thus not really Bible translation, but Bible *interpretation*. The meaning of the text is no longer solely dependent on the original text itself, it is now also made dependent on the thinking of the translator. In dynamic equivalency, "the translator's job is to create a lively Bible by his clever rephrasing of Scripture into colloquial language. Equivalency no longer means that the translator strives as perfectly as possible for an equal transfer of the words and structure of the original. Rather, the emphasis is on a general equivalency, with the translator having great freedom to restate, change, add to, and take away from the original writings" (David W Cloud, *Dynamic Equivalency: Death Knell of Pure Scripture* [Oak Harbor WA: Way of Life Literature, nd], 4).

How does the dynamic equivalence method work? A revealing example may be found in the *Good News For Modern Man* or the *Today's English Version* (1966): By using the dynamic equivalence method, the TEV leaves out the word 'blood' (Greek: *haima*) in no less than 10 places when it refers to the blood of Christ (Acts 20:28; Rom 3:25, 5:9; Eph 1:7, 2:13; Col 1:14, 20; 1 Pet 1:19; Rev 1:5, 5:9). In the name of dynamic equivalence, they have changed what is specifically and literally "blood" to "death," or some other word. 1 Pet 1:18–19 reads: "Forasmuch as ye know that ye were not redeemed with corruptible things, as silver and gold, from your vain conversation received by tradition from your fathers; But with the precious blood of Christ, as of a lamb without blemish and without spot." It is important for us to understand that we are not simply saved by the death of Christ, but the death of Christ which involves the shedding of His precious blood. If Jesus had died by drowning or strangulation, His death would be of no value. The blood is a very important element in the doctrine of the atonement. "There is a fountain filled with blood, drawn from Immanuel's veins, and sinners plunged beneath that flood, lose all their guilty stains." By removing the word "blood" in those places, the TEV has effectively taken away the significance of the blood of Christ for our salvation.

William Tyndale on Accurate Translating

"I call God to record against the day we shall appear before our Lord Jesus, to give a reckoning of our doings, that *I never altered one syllable of God's Word* against my conscience, nor would this day, if all that is in the earth, whether it be pleasure, honour, or riches, might be given me."

HOW WE GOT OUR BIBLE (KJV)

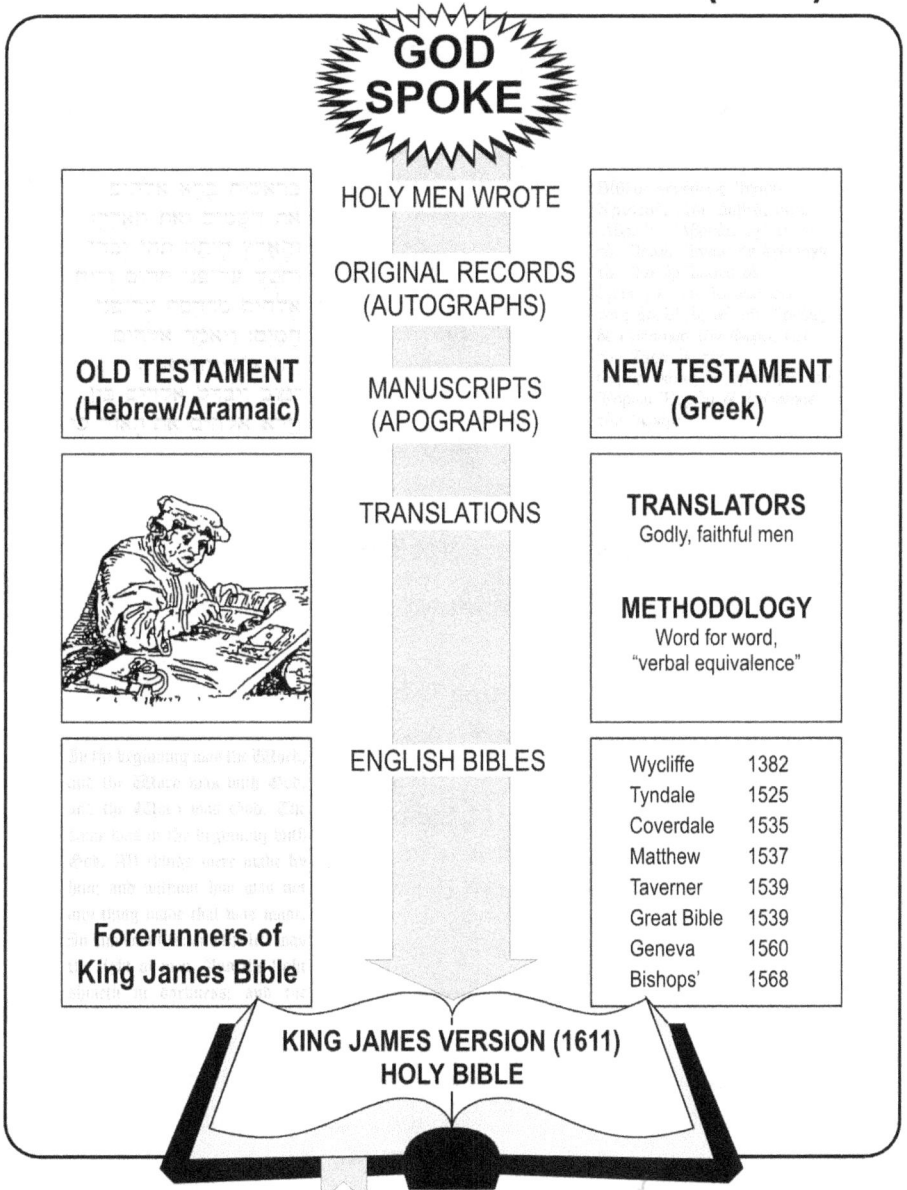

GOD SPOKE

HOLY MEN WROTE

ORIGINAL RECORDS
(AUTOGRAPHS)

**OLD TESTAMENT
(Hebrew/Aramaic)**

MANUSCRIPTS
(APOGRAPHS)

**NEW TESTAMENT
(Greek)**

TRANSLATIONS

TRANSLATORS
Godly, faithful men

METHODOLOGY
Word for word,
"verbal equivalence"

ENGLISH BIBLES

**Forerunners of
King James Bible**

Wycliffe	1382
Tyndale	1525
Coverdale	1535
Matthew	1537
Taverner	1539
Great Bible	1539
Geneva	1560
Bishops'	1568

**KING JAMES VERSION (1611)
HOLY BIBLE**

THE GREEK TEXT OF THE NEW TESTAMENT

CHAPTER VII

THE GREEK TEXT OF THE NEW TESTAMENT

The heat of the debate over the Bible versions has to do primarily with the Greek Text. The KJV is based on the Traditional Text, while most modern versions are based on the Critical Text. Till today, there are two clear-cut attitudes toward the Greek Text: the (1) Pro-Critical/ Westcott-Hort Text, and (2) Pro-Traditional/Received Text attitude. There are a lot of differences between these two texts and attitudes. Which Greek Text best represents the apostolic autographs? Is it the Traditional Text or the Critical Text? Which attitude faithfully promotes a reverent and faithful study of the Scriptures?

The Manuscript Text-type

Generally speaking, the extant NT manuscripts fall into two broad categories:

Byzantine Text-type

This text is also called the Traditional Text or the Majority Text. Westcott and Hort pejoratively labelled it the Syrian Text. This text family is found in the majority of the manuscripts. It is the text-type on which the Textus Receptus or Received Text is based. More than 90% of extant manuscripts agree with the TR. This is the text underlying the KJV.

Alexandrian Text-type

This text family is numerically small, chiefly represented by the Codices Sinaiticus and Vaticanus which are allegedly the earliest and most reliable manuscripts we have today. This is the text on which the modern translations, like the NIV, are based.

The Critical Text

This text is also called the Westcott-Hort Text, the Neutral Text, or the Eclectic Text, and is represented in published form by the United Bible Societies' *Greek New Testament* edited by Kurt Aland, Matthew Black, Carlo M Martini, Bruce Metzger, and Allen Wikgren (UBSGNT), and the Nestle-Aland *Novum Testamentum Graece* (NANTG).

How did this text come about? G W Anderson offers a succinct introduction: "During the 19th and 20th centuries ... another form of Greek New Testament has come into the forefront and is used for most modern New Testament translations. This Critical Text, as it is called, differs widely from the Traditional Text in that it omits many words, verses and passages which are found in the Received Text and translations based upon it.

"The modern versions are based mainly upon a Greek New Testament which was derived from a small handful of Greek manuscripts from the 4th century onwards. Two of these manuscripts, which many modern scholars claim to be superior to the Byzantine are the Sinai manuscript and the Vatican manuscript (c. 4th century). These are derived from a text-type known as the Alexandrian text (because of its origin in Egypt); this text-type was referred to by the textual critics Westcott and Hort as the 'Neutral Text'. These two manuscripts form the basis of the Greek New Testament, referred to as the Critical Text, which has been in widespread use since the late 19th century. In recent years there has been an attempt to improve this text by calling it an 'eclectic text' (meaning that many other manuscripts were consulted in its editing and evolution), but it is still a text which has as its central foundation these two manuscripts" (*The Greek New Testament*, [London: Trinitarian Bible Society, 1994], 2).

The Alexandrian Manuscripts

These manuscripts originate from the Egyptian capital city of Alexandria. Alexandria is mentioned in Acts 6:9 where Stephen debated with the Jews from Alexandria who questioned the deity of Christ, and in Acts 18:24 we are introduced to Apollos who, though highly educated and knowledgeable of the OT, had a very shallow understanding of who Christ really was, and had to be taught and corrected by a Christian lay couple—Aquila and Priscilla. The Scripture seems not to place

Alexandria in a good light. In the fourth century, Arius, a pastor in Alexandria, denied the eternality of Christ, and taught that Jesus had a beginning by misinterpreting the term "only begotten" (John 1:14,18, 3:16). There was at least one shining testimony in Alexandria, namely, Athanasius, Bishop of Alexandria, who opposed Arius and his heresy.

Codex Sinaiticus (א)

"In the year 1844, ... in quest of manuscripts, Tischendorf reached the Convent of St. Catherine, on Mount Sinai. Here observing some old-looking documents in a basketful of papers ready for lighting the stove, he picked them out, and discovered ... a complete New Testament, a large portion of the Septuagint, the Epistle of St. Barnabas, and a fragment of the Shepherd of Hermas. After this, he was allowed to copy the manuscript, and the Codex was in course of time presented to the Emperor. ...

"Before the discovery of this [so called] important manuscript, Tischendorf had issued seven editions of his Greek Testament. ... The eighth edition was constructed with the help of the newly discovered Sinaitic manuscript (א) and his attachment to the treasure that he had rescued proved too much for him. He altered his seventh edition in no less than 3,369 instances, generally in compliance with the Sinaitic copy, 'to the scandal,' as Dr. Scrivener justly remarks, 'of the science of Comparative Criticism, as well as his own discredit for discernment and accuracy.' ... we cannot regard him [Tischendorf] as a man of sober and solid judgment. His zigzag course does not impress us with the soundness of any position upon which he found himself throughout it" (Edward Miller, *A Guide to the Textual Criticism of the New Testament* [Collingswood NJ: Dean Burgon Society, 1979 reprint], 24–5).

"Note that this manuscript, which has so powerfully influenced the men who developed modern textual critical theories, was discovered in a waste paper basket in an Orthodox monastery. Even the benighted monks dwelling in this demonically oppressed place counted it only worthy of burning! Dr. James Qurollo observes, 'I don't know which of them had the truer evaluation of its worth—Tischendorf, who wanted to buy it, or the monks, who were getting ready to burn it!'

"It is important to note that the Sinaiticus shows plain evidence of corruption. Dr. F.H.A. Scrivener, who published in 1864 *A Full*

Collation of the Codex Sinaiticus, testified: 'The Codex is covered with alterations of an obviously correctional character—brought in by at least ten different revisers, some of them systematically spread over every page, ... many of these being contemporaneous with the first writer" (David W Cloud, *Modern Versions Founded Upon Apostasy* [Oak Harbor WA: Way of Life Literature, 1995], 17).

Codex Vaticanus (B)

"As its name shows, [the Vaticanus] is in the Great Vatican Library at Rome, which has been its home since some date before 1481. ... A correspondent of Erasmus in 1533 sent that scholar a number of selected readings from it, ... Napoleon carried the manuscript off as a prize of victory to Paris, where it remained till 1815, when the many treasures of which he had despoiled the libraries of the Continent were returned to their respective owners. ... In 1843 Tischendorf, after waiting for several months, was allowed to see it for six hours. ... In 1845 ... Tregelles was allowed indeed to see it but not to copy a word. His pockets were searched before he might open it, and all writing materials were taken away. Two clerics stood beside him and snatched away the volume if he looked too long at any passage! ... In 1866 Tischendorf once more applied for permission to edit the MS., but with difficulty obtained leave to examine it for the purpose of collating difficult passages. ... Renewed entreaty procured him six days' longer study, making in all fourteen days of three hours each; and by making the very most of his time Tischendorf was able in 1867 to publish the most perfect edition of the manuscript which had yet appeared. An improved Roman edition appeared in 1868–81 ..." (Frederic Kenyon, *Our Bible and the Ancient Manuscripts*, 4th ed [New York: Harper & Brothers, 1939], 138–9).

Cloud rightly observed, "Kenyon's idea that Tischendorf could publish a satisfactory edition of Vaticanus after having examined it for only 42 hours under the above conditions must be some sort of joke! Even the so-called improved edition was carelessly produced, as a number of textual scholars have pointed out" (Cloud, *Modern Versions Founded Upon Apostasy*, 19).

These two Alexandrian manuscripts are absolutely unreliable. Dean Burgon wrote, "B and ℵ, have ... established a tyrannical ascendency over the imagination of the Critics, which can only be fitly spoken of as a blind superstition. It matters nothing that all four are discovered on careful scrutiny to differ essentially, not only from ninety-nine out of a hundred of the whole body of extant MSS. besides, but even *from one another*. This last circumstance, obviously fatal to their corporate pretensions, is unaccountably overlooked. And yet it admits of only one satisfactory explanation: viz. that *in different degrees* they all exhibit a fabricated text. Between the first two (B and ℵ) there subsists an amount of sinister resemblance, which proves that they must have been derived at no very remote period from the same corrupt original. ... And be it remembered that the omissions, additions, substitutions, transpositions, and modifications, *are by no means the same in both*. It is in fact *easier to find two consecutive verses in which these two MSS. differ the one from the other, than two consecutive verses in which they entirely agree*."

"ℵ B ... are ... most scandalously corrupt copies extant:—exhibit the most shamefully mutilated texts which are anywhere to be met with:—have become by whatever process (for their history is wholly unknown), the depositories of the largest amount of fabricated readings, ancient blunders, and intentional perversions of Truth,—which are discoverable in any known copies of the Word of God" (J W Burgon, *The Revision Revised* [Collingswood NJ: Dean Burgon Society Press, 1883], 12,16).

Proof of Corruption

Let me just cite one demonstration by Dean Burgon of the corruption in the 5 uncials Westcott-Hort considered to be most reliable. These 5 uncials are codices: (1) Sinaiticus (ℵ), (2) Alexandrinus (A), (3) Vaticanus (B), (4) Ephraemi Rescriptus (C), and (5) Bezae Cantabrigiensis (D). The passage being examined is the Lord's Prayer in Luke 11:2–4. The results are as follows:

(1) D inserts Matt 6:7, "Use not vain repetitions as the rest: for some suppose that they shall be heard by their much speaking. But when ye pray ...".

(2) B and ℵ removed 5 words "Our," and "which art in heaven."

The Lord's Prayer (Luke 11:2–4)

KJV

And he said unto them, When ye pray, say, Our Father which art in heaven, Hallowed be thy name. Thy kingdom come. Thy will be done, as in heaven, so in earth. Give us day by day our daily bread. And forgive us our sins; for we also forgive every one that is indebted to us. And lead us not into temptation; but deliver us from evil.

Codex Sinaiticus (א)

And he said unto them, When ye pray, say, Father, Hallowed be thy name. Thy kingdom come. Thy will be done, as in heaven, so also in earth *(omits article)*. Give *(form changed)* us day by day *(omits article)* our daily bread. And forgive us our sins; *as also [we] ourselves* forgive every one that is indebted to us. And lead us not into temptation.

Codex Alexandinus (A)

And he said unto them, When ye pray, say, Our Father which art in heaven, Hallowed be thy name. Thy kingdom come. Thy will be done, as in heaven, *so also* in earth *(omits article)*. Give us day by day our daily bread. And forgive us our sins; for we also forgive every one that is indebted to us. And lead us not into temptation; but deliver us from evil.

Codex Vaticanus (B)

And he said unto them, When ye pray, say, Father, Hallowed be thy name. Thy kingdom come. Give us day by day our daily bread. And forgive us our sins; for we also forgive every one that is indebted to us. And lead us not into temptation.

Codex Ephraemi Rescriptus (C)

And he said unto them, When ye pray, say, Our Father which art in heaven, Hallowed be thy name. Thy kingdom come. Thy will be done, as in heaven, *so also* in earth *(omits article)*. Give us day by day our daily bread. And forgive us our sins; for we also forgive every one that is indebted to us. And lead us not into temptation; but deliver us from evil.

Codex Cezae Cantabrigiensis (D)

And he said unto them, *Use not vain repetitions as the rest: for some suppose that they shall be heard by their much speaking; but* when ye pray, say, Our Father which art in heaven, Hallowed be thy name *(omits article)*. Thy kingdom *(words rearranged)* come *upon us*. Thy will be done, as in heaven, so also in earth *(omits article)*. Give *(form changed)* us *this day* our daily bread. And forgive us our *debts; as also* we forgive *our debtors*. And lead us not into temptation; but deliver us from evil.

NIV

He said to them, "When you pray say: 'Father, hallowed be your name, your kingdom come. Give us each day our daily bread. Forgive us our sins, for we also forgive everyone who sins against us. And lead us not into temptation.'"

(3) D omits the definite article "the" before "name," adds "upon us," and rearranges "Thy Kingdom."

(4) B removes the clause, "Thy will be done, as in heaven, also on the earth." Interestingly, ℵ retains these words, but adds "so" before "also," and omits the article before "earth" agreeing for once with A, C, and D.

(5) ℵ and D changed the form of the Greek word for "give."

(6) ℵ omits definite article before "day by day."

(7) D, instead of the 3 last-named words, writes "this day" (from Matt), substitutes "debts" for "sins" (also from Matt), and in place of "for we ourselves" writes "as also we" (again from Matt).

(8) ℵ shows great sympathy with D by accepting two-thirds of this last blunder, exhibiting "as also [we] ourselves."

(9) D consistently read "our debtors" in place of "every one that is indebted to us."

(10) B and ℵ canceled the last petition "but deliver us from evil," going against A, C, and D.

Dean Burgon rightly judged, "So then, these five 'first-class authorities' are found to throw themselves into *six different combinations* in their departures from S. Luke's way of exhibiting the Lord's Prayer,—which, among them, they contrive to falsify in respect of no less than 45 words; and yet *they are never able to agree among themselves as to any single various reading*: while *only once* are more than two of them observed to stand together,—viz. in the unauthorized omission of the article. In respect of 32 (out of the 45) words, *they bear in turn solitary evidence*. What need to declare that it is *certainly false* in every instance? Such however is the infatuation of the Critics, that the vagaries of B are all taken for gospel. Besides omitting the 11 words which B omits jointly with ℵ, Drs. Westcott and Hort erase from the Book of Life those other 11 precious words which are omitted by B only. And in this way it comes to pass that the mutilated condition to which the scalpel of Marcion the heretic reduced the Lord's Prayer some 1730 years ago, (for mischief can all be traced back to *him!*), is palmed off on the Church of England by the Revisionists as the work of the Holy Ghost!" (*Revision Revised*, 34–6).

The Westcott-Hort Text

Their Critical Edition of the Greek NT

Origin and Nature of the Critical Text

"The year 1881 was marked by the publication of the most noteworthy [untrustworthy] critical edition of the Greek Testament ever produced by British scholarship. Brooke Foss Westcott (1825–1901), and Fenton John Anthony Hort (1828–92) issued two volumes entitled, *The New Testament in the Original Greek*. [By] utilizing previous collections of variant readings, they refined the critical methodology developed by Griesbach, Lachmann [German modernists], and others, and applied it rigorously, but with discrimination, to the witnesses to the text of the New Testament... The [so-called] Neutral Text is, in the opinion of Westcott and Hort, most free from later corruption and mixture, and comes nearest to the text of the autographs. It is best represented by codex Vaticanus (B), and next by codex Sinaiticus (ℵ). [According to them] the concurrence of these two manuscripts are very strong, and cannot be far from the original text" (Bruce Metzger, *The Text of the New Testament*, 2nd ed [New York: Oxford University Press, 1968], 129, 133; words in parenthesis mine).

Problems in the Critical Text

Many verses and passages found in the writings of the Church Fathers of the second and third centuries are missing in the Alexandrian manuscripts of the Critical Text. What is significant is that these readings absent in the Alexandrian manuscripts are found in the majority of manuscripts which date from the fifth century onwards. One example is Mark 16:9–20. This passage is cited by early Church Fathers Irenaeus and Hippolytus (2nd century), and is in almost every manuscript of Mark's Gospel from AD 500 onwards, but missing in the Vaticanus and Sinaiticus.

The Critical Text differs from the Traditional Text in over 5,000 places. The Vaticanus omits 2,877 words in the gospels, and the Sinaiticus, even more, 3455. "Westcott and Hort, published their Greek text that rejected the *Textus Receptus* in 5,604 places. ... This included 9,970 Greek words that were either added, subtracted, or changed from the *Textus Receptus*. This involves, on the average, 15.4 words per page in the Greek New Testament, or a total of 45.9 pages in all. It is 7% of the total of 140,521 words in the *Textus Receptus* Greek New Testament (Waite, *Defending the King James Bible*, 40). These omissions do affect doctrine and faith. For example, the Critical Text omits the deity of Christ in 1 Tim 3:16: WH: *Hos ephanerothe en sarki* (NIV: "**He** appeared in a body"); TR: *Theos ephanerothe en sarki* (KJV: "**God** was manifest in the flesh").

Dean Burgon has convincingly proven that the manuscripts Westcott and Hort hailed to be almost like the autographs are among the most corrupt copies of the NT in existence (for in-depth study, read J W Burgon, *The Revision Revised: A Refutation of Westcott and Hort's False Greek Text and Theory* [Collingswood NJ: Dean Burgon Society Press, nd], 1–110). The Revised Version (1881) was substantially based on the Westcott-Hort Text. The RV has not stood the test of time. Although still printed by Cambridge University Press, it is no longer popular.

Their Textual Critical Theory

Premise of the Critical Theory

The basic premise of Westcott and Hort's theory of textual criticism is that the oldest manuscripts are the most accurate or reliable. "In the 1860's the Codex Sinaiticus and Codex Vaticanus became available to Biblical scholars, and in 1881 Westcott and Hort advanced the theory that the New Testament text was preserved in an almost perfect state in these two fourth century manuscripts. ...

"Westcott and Hort devised an elaborate theory, based more on imagination and intuition than upon evidence, elevating this little group of MSS to the heights of almost infallible authority. Their treatise on the subject and their edition of the Greek N.T. exercised a powerful and far-reaching influence, not only on the next generation of students and scholars, but also indirectly upon the minds of millions who have had neither the ability, nor the time, nor the inclination to submit the theory to a searching examination" (*The Divine Original* [London: Trinitarian Bible Society, nd], 4).

In their own words, Westcott and Hort theorised, "it is our belief (1) that readings of ℵB should be accepted as the true readings until strong internal evidence is found to the contrary, and (2) that no readings of B can safely be rejected absolutely, ... especially where they

THE ENTRANCE OF THE LEAVEN OF TEXTUAL CRITICISM INTO FUNDAMENTALISM

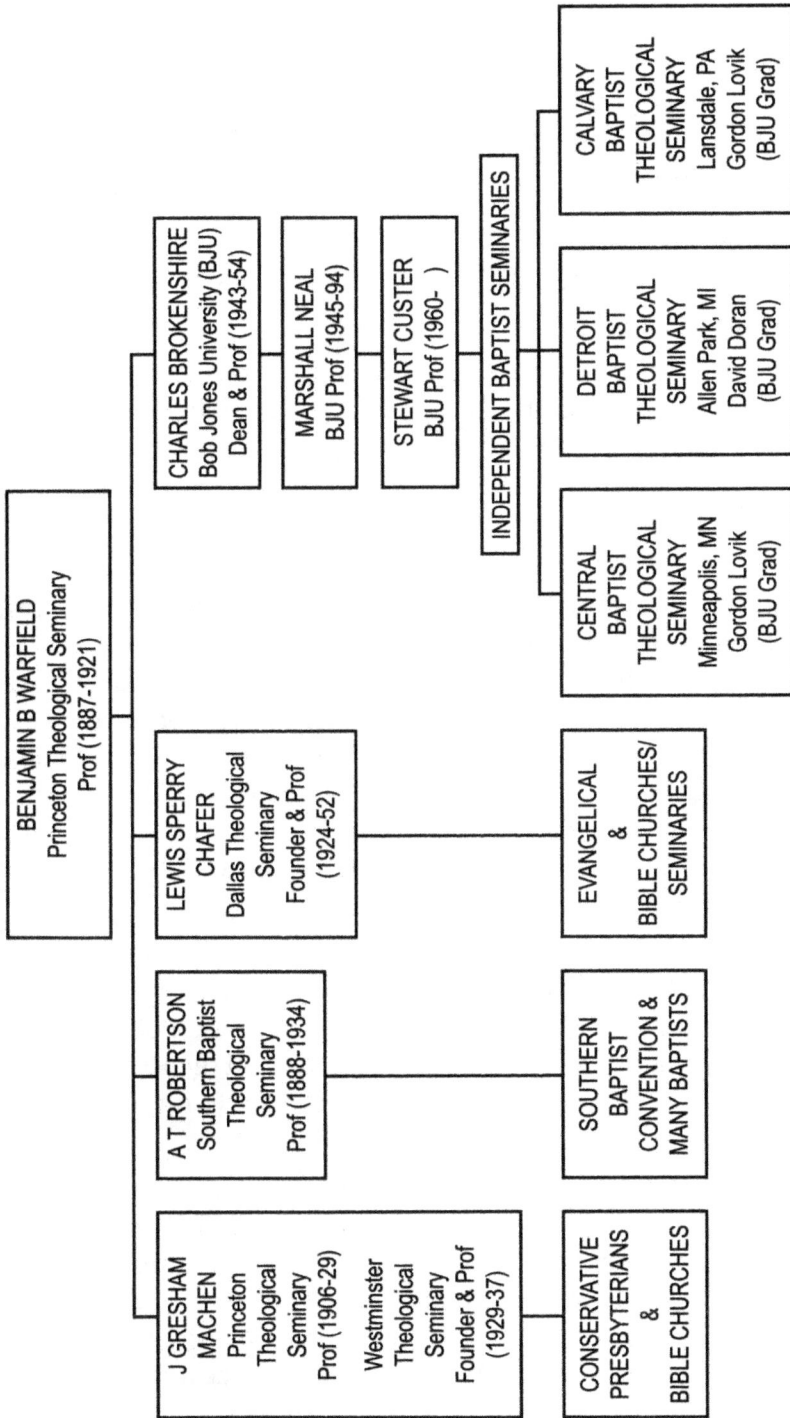

BENJAMIN B WARFIELD
Princeton Theological Seminary
Prof (1887-1921)

J GRESHAM MACHEN
Princeton Theological Seminary
Prof (1906-29)
Westminster Theological Seminary
Founder & Prof (1929-37)

CONSERVATIVE PRESBYTERIANS & BIBLE CHURCHES

A T ROBERTSON
Southern Baptist Theological Seminary
Prof (1888-1934)

SOUTHERN BAPTIST CONVENTION & MANY BAPTISTS

LEWIS SPERRY CHAFER
Dallas Theological Seminary
Founder & Prof (1924-52)

EVANGELICAL & BIBLE CHURCHES/ SEMINARIES

CHARLES BROKENSHIRE
Bob Jones University (BJU)
Dean & Prof (1943-54)

MARSHALL NEAL
BJU Prof (1945-94)

STEWART CUSTER
BJU Prof (1960-)

INDEPENDENT BAPTIST SEMINARIES

CENTRAL BAPTIST THEOLOGICAL SEMINARY
Minneapolis, MN
Gordon Lovik
(BJU Grad)

DETROIT BAPTIST THEOLOGICAL SEMINARY
Allen Park, MI
David Doran
(BJU Grad)

CALVARY BAPTIST THEOLOGICAL SEMINARY
Lansdale, PA
Gordon Lovik
(BJU Grad)

Source: Dell G Johnson, overhead chart entitled "The Leaven in Fundamentalism," in *The Leaven in Fundamentalism: A History of the Bible Text Issue in Fundamentalism*, videocassette tape 3, 145 mins, Pensacola Christian College, 1998. Used by permission.

receive no support from Versions or Fathers" (B F Westcott and F J A Hort, *Introduction to the New Testament in the Original Greek* [New York: Harper and Brothers, 1882], 225).

Based on their theory that ℵ and B are superior, they omit such precious passages as the *pericope de adultera* (John 7:53–8:11), the last twelve verses of Mark, and the Johannine *comma* (1 John 5:7f). In fact, the number of verses taken out of the Bible amounts to that of 1–2 Peter.

Critique of the Critical Theory

There is a fundamental error in Westcott and Hort's textual critical theory. The error lies in "the assumption that the reliability of these 4th century documents was in proportion to their age. There were no doubt bad copies in every age, some corrupted by accident, some by ignorance and some by design. These two exhibit the most amazing number of incorrect readings.

"These two MSS and a few others containing a similar text present in a weakened form many of the passages of Holy Scripture which speak most plainly of the deity of the Son of God. The trend of Biblical scholarship in the 19th and 20th centuries has been towards a 'humanitarian' view of the person of Christ. It does not surprise us that many modern scholars should welcome the support of these two ancient documents, but it saddens us to see so many earnest evangelical Christians ready to accept without question a theory so destructive of the faith once delivered to the saints.

"In the words of a great 19th century scholar, 'To cast away at least nineteen-twentieths of the evidence, and to draw conclusions from the petty remainder is not less than a crime and a sin, not only by reasons of the sacrilegious destructiveness exercised upon the Holy Scriptures, but because such a treatment is inconsistent with conscientious exhaustiveness and logical method.'

"The Sinai and Vatican manuscripts represent a small family of documents containing various readings which the Church as a whole rejected before the end of the 4th century. Under the singular care and providence of God more reliable MSS were multiplied and copied from generation to generation, and the great majority of existing MSS exhibit a faithful reproduction of the true text which was acknowledged by the entire Greek Church in the Byzantine period A.D. 312–1453. This text was also represented by the small group of documents available to Erasmus, Stephens, the compilers of the Complutension edition of other 16th century editors. This text is represented by the Authorised Version and other Protestant translations up to the latter part of the 19th century" (*The Divine Original*, 5).

Their Heretical Beliefs

Denial of the Historicity of the Creation Account

Hort supported Darwin's theory of evolution: "But the book which has most engaged me is Darwin. Whatever may be thought of it, it is a book that one is proud to be contemporary with. I must work out and examine the argument in more detail, but at present my feeling is strong that the theory is unanswerable" (Hort, *Life*, I:416).

Westcott believed the first three chapters of Genesis to be mythical: "No one now, I suppose, holds that the first three chapters of Genesis, for example, give a literal history. I could never understand how any one reading them with open eyes could think they did" (Westcott, *Life*, I:78).

Denial of the Sole Mediatorship of Christ

Hort acknowledged the worship of Mary is legitimate: "I have been persuaded for many years that Mary-worship and 'Jesus'-worship have very much in common in their causes and their results" (Hort, *Life*, II:50).

Westcott took delight in Mary-worship and idolatry: "After leaving the monastery, we shaped our course to a little oratory which we discovered on the summit of a neighbouring hill. ... Fortunately we found the door opened. It is very small, with one kneeling place; and behind a screen was a 'Pieta' the size of life (i.e. a Virgin and dead Christ]. ... Had I been alone I could have knelt there for hours" (Westcott, *Life*, I:81).

The Eclectic Text

With the entrance of the Westcott-Hort (WH) edition of the Greek NT, the foundation of the systematic corruption of the Bible has been laid. Since that time, modern Bible scholars have echoed Westcott and

Hort, writing off the TR/KJV as unreliable and outdated. They pushed for new translations of the Bible. Among other lesser known ones, the Revised Standard Version (RSV, 1952), New American Standard Bible (NASB, 1971), and New International Version (NIV, 1978) have been the key players in following the WH philosophy of textual criticism and Bible translation.

Westcott and Hort and Modern Evangelical Scholarship

Harold Greenlee commented, "All things considered, the influence of WH upon all subsequent work in the history of the text has never been equalled. … With the work of Westcott and Hort the T.R. was at last vanquished … [and] the textual theory of WH underlies virtually all subsequent work in N.T. textual criticism" (*Introduction to New Testament Textual Criticism* [Grand Rapids MI: Wm B Eerdmans, 1964], 77–8).

D A Carson confessed, "the vast majority of evangelical scholars … hold that in the basic textual theory Westcott and Hort were right, and that the church stands greatly in their debt" (*The King James Version Debate* [Grand Rapids MI: Baker Book House, 1979], 75).

Legacy of Westcott and Hort in Modern Editions of the Greek NT

Unable to refute the arguments leveled against the WH text and theory, anti-KJVists attempt to distance themselves from WH by arguing that modern English translations are not based on WH. One NIV-advocate for instance pointed out that the NIV is not based on the WH text but an "eclectic" text. It is true that the NIV claims to be based on a so-called eclectic text: "The Greek text used in translating the New Testament was an eclectic one. … Where existing manuscripts differ, the translators made their choice of readings according to accepted principles of New Testament textual criticism. … The best current printed texts of the Greek New Testament were used" (NIV "Preface").

The NIV translators say they use an eclectic text, and then a few sentences down, they say that the best current printed Greek NT texts were used. Questions: (1) What is the eclectic text? (2) Who edited and published this text? (3) Which are the best current printed texts of the Greek NT? (4) Is the eclectic text actually the best current printed texts of the Greek NT? (5) What "accepted" principles of NT textual criticism were employed? It will be seen that the NIV (representative of the

B F Westcott
(1825–1901)

F J A Hort
(1828–1892)

The DEADLY DUO from Cambridge, Westcott and Hort, harbouring inner hatred for the Biblical faith and a secret love for Rome and Mary Worship, posed as "evangelicals," and using the corrupt Codex Vaticanus and Codex Sinaiticus, gave the world their Westcott and Hort Greek NT, which ever since has received global acceptance as "the most accurate, authentic and trustworthy."

Both Westcott and Hort, whether jointly or individually, had denied every fundamental doctrine of the evangelical faith, proving that they were both strangers to the saving grace of God, and enemies of the Gospel of our Lord Jesus Christ.

Yet these unregenerate men applied their unholy hands to God's Holy Word. Against such our Lord has a warning, ". . . *a corrupt tree bringeth forth evil fruit*" (Matt 7:15–18). Out of their evil fruit, the WH Greek NT, came a multitude of "evil fruits"—a hundred New English versions and perversions—a corrupt tree cannot bring forth good fruit.

modern versions) has its roots in the WH text and textual critical theory. As admitted in the NIV preface, the best printed editions of the Greek NT available today were used; the "best ones" in their view being those published by the United Bible Societies and Deutsche Bibelgesellschaft. These are the "scholarly" editions. The other printed edition of the Greek NT is none other than the venerable *Textus Receptus* which modern scholars, parotting WH, consider inferior.

The United Bible Societies' Greek New Testament (UBSGNT)

The UBSGNT is founded on the WH text. The preface to its first edition states, "The Committee carried out its work ... on the basis of Westcott and Hort's edition of the Greek New Testament." It is significant to note that the first and second editions relegated John 7:53–8:11 from its original and traditional place, to the end of the Gospel. This to show that the passage is considered non-authentic. This clearly reveals a WH attitude in accepting without question the testimony of ℵ and B which do not have the pericope of the woman taken in adultery. The third edition however transposed "the pericope John 7.53–8.11 from the end of the Gospel to its traditional location, with the double brackets retained." Perhaps the editors are now admitting their error in rejecting the pericope. In any case, the double brackets are retained. What do these double brackets mean? "Double brackets in the text indicate that the enclosed passages which are usually rather extensive, are known not to be a part of the original text" (Barbara Aland, Kurt Aland, Johannes Karavidopoulos, Matthew Black, Carlo M Martini, Bruce M Metzger, and Allen Wikgren, eds, *The Greek New Testament*, 4th rev ed [Stuttgart: United Bible Societies, 1994]). They still refuse to accept the authenticity of the pericope.

The Nestle-Aland Greek New Testament (NANTG)

The NANTG is exactly the same as the UBSGNT except for its fuller critical apparatus. It is said the UBSGNT is meant for the translator, while the NANTG for the exegete (NANTG27, 45*). The NANTG like the UBSGNT owes a great deal to the WH text: "It is well known how he [Eberhard Nestle] compared the editions of Tischendorf, Westcott and Hort, and Weymouth" (Ibid, 44*). Nestle himself admits that his text is heavily influenced by Westcott and Hort. The "origin of the text itself was clearly traceable ... particularly in passages where the special theories of Westcott-Hort had dominant influence in its formation" (NANTG26, 39). It is thus no surprise that Mark 16:9–20 and John 7:53–8:11 are also assigned double brackets to indicate their non-genuineness as in the UBSGNT.

Vestiges of Westcott and Hort in Modern Versions of the English Bible

NIV-advocates say that it is erroneous to connect the NIV with Westcott and Hort. To do so invites the ridicule of engaging in scholarship of the steamship age. Are KJV supporters really so out of touch with the so-called advances of Biblical scholarship? Actually, to say that the NIV was not influenced whatsoever by Westcott-Hort is denial at its height. Gordon Fee, though a TR/KJV opponent, honestly confessed that *"all* subsequent critical texts [i.e. UBSGNT, NANTG] look far more *like WH* than like the TR" ("The Textual Criticism of the New Testament," in *The Expositor's Bible Commentary*, ed Frank E Gaebelein [Grand Rapids MI: Regency Reference Library, 1979], I:428). And it is on such critical texts that the modern versions are based. G W Anderson of The Trinitarian Bible Society in his booklet—*The Greek Text of the New Testament*—has rightly observed, "In recent years there has been an attempt to improve this text by calling it an 'eclectic' text (meaning that many other manuscripts were consulted in its editing and evolution), but *it is still a text which has as its central foundation these two manuscripts* [i.e. א and B]."

In actual fact, the usage of the term "eclectic" to apply to a text is a misnomer. Actually there is no such thing as an Eclectic Text, but an Eclectic *Method*. What is this method all about? Harry A Sturz explains and critiques, "This method endeavors to have no favorite manuscript and no preferred type of text. ... [However] the eclectic approach, though quite objective in the sense of being willing to consider all readings, is admittedly very subjective in that much depends on the personal element in the evaluation of the evidence. ... textual scholars have given lip-service ... but in practice they do not appear to carry out the theory or the method with consistency, especially with regard to the consideration of Byzantine [Majority Text] readings. Therefore, for all practical purposes, because of the low esteem in which the text is still held by most critics, a Byzantine reading does not generally receive much consideration even under the eclectic method" (*The Byzantine Text-Type and New Testament Criticism* [Nashville TN: Thomas Nelson, 1984], 16–8).

Gordon Fee, who is anti-TR/KJV, himself corrected this confusion: "[In] Modern textual criticism, the 'eclecticism' of the UBS, RSV, NIV, NASB etc., ... *recognizes that Westcott-Hort's view of things was essentially correct*, but it is not nearly so confident as they that the early text of Alexandria is 'neutral'." It is thus clear that Westcott and Hort continue to have a hynoptic hold on modern-day textual critics and Bible translators in terms of their textual critical thinking. Following the lead of Westcott and Hort, the NIV translators took a low view of the Traditional Text having scissored out many precious verses of the Bible. Such an attitude is reflected by J Harold Greenlee who wrote, "the general impression which is given by readings which are characteristically Byzantine is that they are inferior and not likely to be original" (*Introduction to New Testament Criticism*, 91).

Although later editions of the critical text did attempt to move away from the WH text toward an "eclectic" text, it is evident that the vestiges of WH remain. The textual critical methodology of WH for the most part is still being employed by these modern editors. For example, the UBSGNT editors are absolutely certain that the *pericope de adultera* (John 7:53–8:11) is not a part of the Gospel. What is their basis? They say, "the passage is absent from the earlier and better manuscripts" (i.e. Vaticanus and Sinaiticus among other like ones). Note that the same comment against the authenticity of John 7:53–8:11 is found in modern versions like the NIV: the NIV has this note above the passage, "[The earliest and most reliable manuscripts and other ancient witnesses do not have John 7:53–8:11.]" So how can it be concluded that the NIV for instance is not based on WH? Other examples are the last 12 verses of Mark, and 1 John 5:7–8. All decisions made have been consistently against the TR and KJV. We will discuss more about the authenticity of the above passages later on.

The Editors of the Critical Text

It is unfortunate that evangelical and fundamentalist scholars have fallen prey to the views of Westcott and Hort. The masters of the WH tradition were primarily the liberal scholars. Alfred Martin, former vicepresident of Moody Bible Institute, wrote, "At precisely the time when liberalism was carrying the field in the English churches the theory of Westcott and Hort received wide acclaim. There are not isolated facts. Recent contributions on the subject—that is, in the present century— following mainly the Westcott-Hort principles and method, have been made largely by men who deny the inspiration of the Bible" ("A Critical Examination of the Westcott-Hort Textual Theory," ThD diss, Dallas Theological Seminary, 1951, 70). It is surprising then that evangelicals and fundamentalists are so gullible as to become their disciples. Men like A T Robertson, and B B Warfield have unwittingly fallen into the Westcott-Hort trap, leading many of their students into the same. Terence Brown, ex-secretary of the Trinitarian Bible Society, said, "Many liberal and evangelical scholars alike embraced the basic theory of Westcott and Hort and in a very short period, through the colleges, schools and pulpits of the English-speaking world, the theory became embedded in the minds of many, as if it were a proved and demonstrated fact" ("What is Wrong with the Modern Versions of the Holy Scriptures?, Trinitarian Bible Society, article #41).

David Cloud exposes the unbelief and apostasy of the editors of the critical/eclectic text in his book—*Modern Versions Founded Upon Apostasy* (Oak Harbor WA: Way of Life Literature, 1995), 42–50.

Carlo M Martini (1908–2012)

Martini was the Roman Catholic Archbishop of Milan. He was Professor of NT Textual Criticism at the Pontifical Bible Institute in Rome. *TIME* Magazine (Dec 26, '96) listed him as a possible candidate in line for the papacy. Another *TIME* article reported that Martini brought together 100 religious leaders from around the world to promote a new age, one-world religion.

Eugene Nida (1914– 2011)

Nida was the father of the dynamic equivalency theory of Bible translation. As to his view of Bible inspiration, Nida said, "... God's revelation involved limitations. ... Biblical revelation is not absolute and all divine revelation is essentially incarnational. ... Even if a truth is given only in words, it has no real validity until it has been translated into life. ... The words are in a sense nothing in and of themselves. ... the word is void unless related to experience" (*Message and Mission*, 222–8). Nida's view on the inspiration of the Bible is Barthianistic.

Bruce Metzger (1914–2007)

Metzger was Professor of NT at Princeton Theological Seminary. He served on the board of the American Bible Society and was the head of the ecumenical RSV/NRSV translation committee of the apostate National Council of Churches in USA. Metzger was also the chairman for the *Reader's Digest Condensed Bible* or "the Butcher's Bible" because 40% of the Bible has been "chopped off." It is no surprise that the warning of Rev 22:18–19 has also been conveniently deleted in this Bible. Metzger was a modernist who denied the historicity of the book of Genesis, and the uniqueness of the Synoptic Gospels.

Kurt Aland (1915–1994)

Kurt Aland and his wife Barbara were chief editors of the NANTG. Aland had an extremely low view of the TR and the doctrine of Biblical inspiration. He said, "This idea of verbal inspiration (i.e., of the literal and inerrant inspiration of the text), which the orthodoxy of both Protestant traditions maintained so vigorously, was applied to the Textus Receptus with all of its errors, including textual modifications of an obviously secondary character (as we recognize them today)" (*The Problem of the New Testament Canon*, 6–7).

The Traditional Text

What do we mean by the term "traditional text?" The Trinitarian Bible Society explains:

The Byzantine/Majority Text

"During the first century following the resurrection of Christ, God moved men to pen His Word (2 Peter 1.21). The result was a group of letters and books, written in *Koine* Greek (called the 'original autographs'). These letters and books were copied and recopied through the centuries and distributed throughout the world. These copies comprise the manuscripts of the New Testament. Over 5,000 of these Greek manuscripts have survived to this day. The great number of these Greek manuscripts supports what is called the Byzantine textual tradition, Byzantine because it came from all over the Greek-speaking world at that time. These Byzantine manuscripts make up what is called the Traditional Text of the New Testament" (G

W Anderson, *The Greek New Testament* [England: Trinitarian Bible Society, 1994]).

The Textus Receptus/Received Text

"The best printed representation of this Byzantine Text-type is the Textus Receptus (or Received Text). In addition to the manuscripts, we also have available many works in which numerous Church Fathers quoted from the manuscripts. The work of John Burgon has established that the basic text used by numerous Church Fathers is the same as the text now known as the Byzantine Text.

"The Textus Receptus was compiled from a number of Byzantine manuscripts by numerous editors from the early 1500s. There were editions from textual editors such as Erasmus, Stephens, Beza, the Elzevir brothers, Mill and Scrivener. These editions differ slightly from one another but still are regarded as the same basic text. Certain editions were popular in different countries and provided the basis for New Testament translations. The Textus Receptus (as it later became known) was the text used by Tyndale and in turn by the translators of the English Authorised (King James) Version of 1611 and other Reformation era translations" (Ibid).

The Preserved Text

In summary, the Traditional Text is called the Byzantine Text or the Majority Text. It is "Byzantine" because most of the manuscripts originate from the Byzantine empire (i.e. the empire that succeeded the Roman in about AD 300). Moreover, the majority of the extant manuscripts are of the Byzantine text-type. There are slightly over 5,000 extant Greek NT manuscripts, and over 90% of them belong to this text-type. The Byzantine text finds "its chief representative: the Textus Receptus (TR). Most textual students of the New Testament would agree that the TR was made from a few medieval manuscripts, mostly Byzantine" (Sturz, *The Byzantine Text-Type*, 14). That is why Dean Burgon called it the "Traditional" text. Hills who took the same line as Burgon concluded, "therefore the Byzantine text found in the vast majority of the Greek New Testament manuscripts is that true text. To reject this view is to act unreasonably. It is to fly at the facts." Hills continued by chiding those who reject the Majority Text, "Those who reject this orthodox view of the New Testament text have rejected not merely the facts but also the promise of Christ always to preserve the true New Testament text and the doctrines of the divine inspiration and providential preservation of the Scripture implied in this promise" (quoted by Sturz, ibid, 16). The Traditional Text is the text that was used by most of the churches for 1800 years till Tischendorf, Westcott, and Hort came into the picture with their minority text. It can thus also be called the Preserved Text.

The Traditional or Preserved Text is superior because it (1) has been accepted by the churches at large, and (2) can be retraced in history to go all the way back to the original manuscripts of the Greek NT. Dr Waite says, "The Received Text in the New Testament is the [Traditional] Text—the text that has survived in continuity from the beginning of the New Testament itself. It is the only accurate representation of the originals we have today!" (For the historical links, see his book, *Defending the King James Bible*, 44–8).

The "Jesus Papyrus" (Magdalen GR 17)

We have been repeatedly told that the oldest and most reliable manuscripts are the Vaticanus and Sinaiticus codices. They are the best representives of the autographs. The falsity of this claim is evinced in the recent discovery of a papyrus called Magdalen GR 17 kept in Magdalen College, Oxford University. This is reported in the December 1996 issue of the Baptist Reformed Fellowship Journal. In his book—*The Jesus Papyrus*—published by Weidenfeld-Nicolson (England) and Doubleday (New York), Dr Carsten Peter Thiede wrote that the Magdalen GR 17 "is to be dated to a point within the lifetimes of eyewitnesses to Christ. ... This makes the 'Magdalen' papyrus one of the oldest known fragments of the New Testament, and 'one of the most important documents in the world.' " In other words, the papyrus can be dated to about AD 60 or earlier. He concluded this to be so based on the style of handwriting which belonged to that of the mid-first century, similar to the manuscripts found at Qumran. Further, the papyrus was printed on both sides (i.e. front and back), a common printing-form of the first century AD.

The Magdalen GR 17 consists of 3 small fragments, and is a portion of Matthew's Gospel (Matt 26:7–8, 26:10, 14–15, 22–23, 31–33). Among other things, what is significant is the Magdalen's bearing on the identification of the traditional text. Hereunder is the BRF report on "Papyrus Magdalen GR 17 and the Textus Receptus": "In the analysis of GR 17 undertaken under the laser-scanning microscope, certain definite results concerning particular Greek letters that had originally been written on the GR 17 were obtained which enabled the researchers to conclude that the papyrus followed a certain form of textual reading. A comparison of this reading with the 'Post-Westcott-Hort' text of the 27th edition of the Nestle-Aland *Novum Testamentum Graece* indicated a salient difference.

"Authors Thiede and D'Ancona ... point out that GR17 has, on the last 4 words of Matthew 26:22 a reading which is disparate from modern standard critical editions of the Greek New Testament which are of course, all 'Westcott-Hort' based eclectic text, the basis of all modern translations.

"It is apposite therefore at this point to compare GR 17 with a 'Westcott-Hort' reading, and juxtapose both in parallel against the old Textus Receptus."

Last Four Words of Matt 26:22	
Westcott-Hort	*legein auto heis hekastos*
Papyrus GR17	*legein auto hekastos auton*
Textus Receptus	*legein auto hekastos auton*

This is significant. We have here a very early 1st century manuscript which agrees with the Textus Receptus over against the Westcott-Hort Text! This confirms Burgon's observation all along—the Westcott-Hort Text is a corrupted text, the early age of its primary manuscripts notwithstanding.

CHAPTER VIII

A SURVEY OF ENGLISH BIBLE TRANSLATIONS

The books referred to for this section were: (1) F F Bruce, *History of the Bible in English*, 3rd ed (New York: Oxford University Press, 1978); Philip W Comfort, *The Complete Guide to Bible Versions* (Wheaton: Tyndale House, 1991); Jack P Lewis, *The English Bible from KJV to NIV: A History and Evaluation*, 2nd ed (Grand Rapids: Baker Book House, 1991); and Laurence M Vance, *A Brief History of English Bible Translations* (Pensacola: Vance Publications, 1993).

In this study, we will attempt to familiarise ourselves with the major English Bible translations that have been produced. The KJV is really the watershed translation. As such we will divide our discussion on the English Bibles into 2 main periods: pre-KJV and post-KJV. There is significant difference between the versions that came before and those that came after the KJV.

Pre-KJV Versions

Wycliffe's Translation

John Wycliffe (1330–1384) was the most famous Oxford theologian of the 14th century. He was called "The morning star of the Reformation" for his attacks against the heresies of the Roman Catholic Church. The RCC has kept the people in spiritual darkness and bondage by keeping the Bible away from them. He was the first to translate the whole Bible into English. He did this to rescue the people from the tyranny of the Church of Rome. The translation was done not from the Hebrew and Greek, but from the Latin Bible—Jerome's Vulgate. A group of pastors known as the Lollards used Wycliffe's translation to read and preach the Word to the common folk.

Tyndale's Translation

William Tyndale (1494–1536) studied the Hebrew and Greek Scriptures when he was at Oxford University. He completed translating the NT in 1525. 15,000 copies were printed and distributed in England.

The Church of England then under the Roman Catholic Church refused to allow the people to read the English NT. For translating the Scriptures, the Church branded Tyndale a criminal. A warrant was issued for his arrest. In prison, he wrote this letter to the Marquis of Bergen, "I believe, right worshipful, that you are not unaware of what may have been determined concerning me. Wherefore I beg your lordship, and that by the Lord Jesus, that if I am to remain here through the winter, you will request the commissary to have the kindness to send me, from the goods of mine which he has, a warmer cap; for I suffer greatly from cold in the head, am afflicted by a perpetual catarrh, which is much increased in this cell; a warmer coat also, for this which I have is very thin; a piece of cloth too to patch my leggings. My overcoat is worn out; my shirts are also worn out. He has a woollen shirt, if he will be good enough to send it. I have also with him leggings of thicker cloth to put on above; he has also warmer night caps. And I ask to be allowed to have a lamp in the evening; it is indeed wearisome sitting alone in the dark. But most of all I beg and beseech your clemency to be urgent with the commissary that he will kindly permit me to have the Hebrew bible, Hebrew grammar, and Hebrew dictionary, that I may pass the time in that study. In return may you obtain what you most desire, provided that it be consistent with the salvation of your soul. But if any other decision has been taken concerning me, to be carried out before winter, I will be patient, abiding the will of God, to the glory of the grace of my Lord Jesus Christ, whose spirit (I pray) may ever direct your heart. Amen."

Tyndale was later condemned to death. He was strangled and burnt at the stake. His dying words were: "Lord, open the King of England's eyes."

Coverdale's Translation

Myles Coverdale (1488–1569) was a graduate of Cambridge University who became an Augustinian priest. Influenced by the Reformation movement, he broke away from the Roman Catholic Church. From England, he fled to the Continent where he found Tyndale and there helped Tyndale with his translation work. Coverdale continued Tyndale's work and completed translating the Old Testament. The whole Coverdale Bible was completed in 1535.

By that time, the King of England had already broken all ties with Rome, and was eager to see an English Bible. Coverdale's Bible received the king's approval. Tyndale's prayer was answered; the Lord had opened the eyes of the king of England.

The Great Bible

In 1537, another Bible was published in England called the Matthew's Bible. It was the work of Thomas Matthew (1500–55) who was a friend of Tyndale. Thomas Matthew was not a translator but an editor of the Bible. He combined the Tyndale and Coverdale translations to form a complete Bible. Published in 1539, it received the king's authorisation for public use. It is called the Great Bible for its size and cost. The Great Bible was later revised in 1568 and became known as the Bishop's Bible.

The Geneva Bible

The persecution of the reformers by the Roman Catholic Church led many of them to seek refuge in Geneva. It was in that great city that William Whittingham (1524–79)—Calvin's brother-in-law, and Knox's successor as pastor of the English Church in Geneva—translated the NT in what was to become the Geneva Bible. Whittingham used the Textus Receptus (Stephanus' edition), and next to Tyndale became the version that had the most influence on the KJV. The Geneva Bible was both Calvinistic and anti-Catholic. It became very popular with the people because it was inexpensive and handy. The KJV was its successor.

Post-KJV Versions

The KJV has been the undisputed Bible of the English world since 1611. But a turning point came in the late 19th century. It was a period of time when theological liberalism was at its height. Not only were the fundamentals of the Christian Faith being attacked, the Word of God itself was also being altered by men such as Tischendorf, Westcott, and Hort. In 1881, Westcott and Hort produced their edition of the Greek NT. This Greek edition differed greatly from the Greek text underlying the

KJV. It was based on corrupted and unreliable manuscripts, namely, the Codex Sinaiticus and Codex Vaticanus as exposed by Dean Burgon. A multitude of English versions based on the Westcott and Hort text soon followed. Notwithstanding, the KJV still remained the most widely used English Bible. Many of these new versions have died a "diseased death" according to Dr Timothy Tow, but the KJV has stood the test of time and continues to be top on the bestseller's list (however, some reports say that the KJV now occupies 2nd spot behind the NIV).

Revised Version

The RV of 1885 (NT: 1881) was the first version that sought to "correct" the KJV. This was so desired because of the emergence of the new critical text of Westcott and Hort which differed significantly from the Textus Receptus underlying the KJV. The WH Text differed from the TR in 5,604 places. Among those invited to produce the RV were apostates and heretics, namely, (1) Westcott and Hort themselves, (2) John Henry Newman—#1 Roman Catholic theologian in the English-speaking world at that time, (3) G Vance Smith—a Unitarian (i.e. one who denies the doctrine of the Trinity).

In his book—*The Revision Revised* (1883), Dean Burgon ably exposed the errors of the WH Text from which the RV was translated. For example, in the WH Text, Luke 23:34: "Then said Jesus, Father, forgive them; for they know not what they do" is absent; and a marginal note says, "some ancient authorities omit." Burgon, in holy indignation, wrote against this blatant attack on God's Word, "These twelve precious words ... Drs. Westcott and Hort enclose within double brackets in token of the 'moral certainty' they entertain that the words are spurious. And yet these words are found in *every known uncial and in every known cursive Copy, except four; besides being found in every ancient Version*: and, what,— (we ask the question with sincere simplicity),—what amount of evidence is calculated to inspire undoubting confidence in any existing Reading, if not such a concurrence of Authorities as this? ... We forbear to insist upon the probabilities of the case. The Divine power and sweetness of the incident shall not be enlarged upon. We introduce no considerations resulting from Internal Evidence. True, that 'few verses of the Gospels bear in themselves a sure witness to the Truth of what they record, than this.' (It is the admission of the very man [i.e. Dr

Hort] who has nevertheless dared to brand it with suspicion.) But we reject his loathsome patronage with indignation. 'Internal evidence,'— 'Transcriptional Probablity', —and all such 'chaff and draff,' with which he fills his pages *ad nauseam*, and mystifies nobody but himself,—shall be allowed no place in the present discussion" (*Revision Revised*, 82–3).

Other missing verses were John 5:3f, Acts 8:37, and 1 John 5:7. Many readers of the RV were greatly disturbed by the excision of the Trinitarian verse from the Bible. They felt that the doctrine of the Trinity had been undermined. It is no wonder that the RV never caught on, and not surprisingly since gone out of print.

American Standard Version

The ASV of 1901 was a revision or the American edition of the RV. One helpful feature about the ASV is in its paragraph divisions. As with the RV, it did not measure up to the standard set by the KJV, and is cast aside.

Revised Standard Version

The RSV (1952) is a revision of the ASV. It is an ecumenical Bible translated by 32 scholars (this includes a Jewish rabbi) from various modernistic denominations belonging to the National Council of Churches. Read "Rome and the RSV" by Dr Hugh Farrell (Trinitarian Bible Society).

In the original edition of the RSV, John 7:53–8:11 on the woman taken in adultery was taken out from the main text and placed in the margin. The last 12 verses of Mark were excised entirely. Today we have them back in the rightful places. Why?

The RSV of course did not sit very well with the fundamentalists. This was because the RSV made a blatant attack against the virgin birth by rendering the Hebrew 'almah as "young woman" (Isa 7:14). The Virgin Birth of Christ was meant to be a miraculous sign to the house of David. If a young woman conceives, how then can it be a sign? It is a God-given miracle only if a virgin conceives. It is something supernatural and unique. The angel Gabriel quoting Isa 7:14 said that the prophecy of the Virgin Birth was fulfilled in Jesus who came from the womb of Mary, a *parthenos*, "a virgin." Was the angel wrong when he told us that this is the meaning of the word *'almah* in Isa 7:14? No, these so-called scholars of the RSV were in error, not the angel. The angel surely knew Hebrew and Greek much better than they! Matt 1:18 and 25 tell us in no uncertain terms that Mary was a virgin from the time she conceived Jesus till the time she gave birth to Him.

It is no wonder that Rabbi Israel Bettan criticised the RSV. He said of the RSV, "The Revised Standard Version *is not a faithful translation*, and in some places the revisers do violence to the original Hebrew. It is a good book on the Bible, but it *is not the Bible*. When asked to compare the King James Version with various other translations, the rabbi said that of the English versions mentioned the King James Version was, in his opinion, the most faithful to the original" (*The Brethren Missionary Herald* [Feb 1958]). The same is said by Dr Robert Alter (BA, Columbia University, MA, PhD, Harvard University) who was professor of Hebrew at the University of California, Berkeley, "Modern English versions put readers at a grotesque distance from the Hebrew Bible. To this day, the *Authorized Version* of 1611 (the "King James Bible") ... for all its archaisms ... remains the closest we have ... of the original." Bruce Metzger and company produced a revision of the RSV called New RSV (1989). In support of the feminist movement, it has replaced generic masculine nouns/pronouns with gender-inclusive terms.

New English Bible

The NEB (1970) was a British work published by the Oxford and Cambridge University Presses. The translation committee consisted of those from UK Protestant Churches, viz the Church of England, Church of Scotland, the Churches of Wales and Ireland, the Methodist, Baptist, and Congregational churches, and the Society of Friends. Most of the verses relegated to the margin in the WH text are also found only in the margin of the NEB. There are thus missing verse numbers.

The NEB denies that Gen 3:15 (NEB: "I will put enmity between you and the woman, between your brood and hers. They shall strike at your head, and you shall strike at their heel.") is the first gospel divinely predictive of the virgin-born Messiah. Look at the NEB's corruption of Gen 3:15: (1) "thy seed and her seed" is changed to "your brood and hers," and (2) The singular "it" (he) is changed to "they;" and "his" is changed to "their." Why? There can be no other reason but to deny that Gen 3:15 is Messianic, divinely predictive of the Lord Jesus Christ.

It also attacked the prophecy of the virgin birth in Isa 7:14 following the steps of the RSV. The NEB translates the word "virgin" as "a young woman is with child."

Today's English Version or Good News for Modern Man

The NT of the TEV (1966) was translated by Robert Bratcher, and published by the American Bible Society. The complete Bible came out in 1976 and was renamed the Good News Bible (GNB).

The TEV/GNB attacks the blood of Christ. In 10 places the word "blood" has been replaced by the word "death" (Acts 20:28, Rom 3:25, 5:9, Eph 1:7, 2:13, Col 1:14, 20, 1 Pet 1:19, Rev 1:5, 5:9). The Greek *haima* means "blood" not "death." If Jesus' death was a bloodless one, it would have been in vain, for "without shedding of blood there is no remission" (Heb 9:22 cf 1 Pet 1:19).

The TEV/GNB employed the dynamic equivalence method of translation. Dr Tan Wai Choon criticised the TEV: "a translation of this type is not really a translation at all but a paraphrase and commentary. Very little of the TEV (*i.e. the Good News Bible*) is literal. Almost every verse has been injected with the opinion of the translator as to what he thinks the Greek text means, rather than what it says. ... Aside from its basic failure to provide a literal translation, it is simply not accurate" ("What's Wrong with the Good News Bible?" FEBC Press, nd, np). *The sound criticism above applies equally to the NIV which adopts the same erroneous method of translating Scripture.* It is unfortunate that Dr Tan in the same article promoted the NIV. In so doing, he contradicted himself.

Living Bible

The *Living Bible* (1971) was translated by Kenneth Taylor. It was not a translation of the original text, but a paraphrasing of the ASV. According to Taylor, paraphrasing is "to say something in different words than the author used. It is a restatement of the author's thoughts, using different words than he did." This is a most unacceptable method of translating the Scriptures. It is deceptive to name it the "Living Bible." It is neither "Bible" nor "Living." Such a paraphrase should be called "The

Deadly Bible." I heard a prominent Bible professor at an ETS (Evangelical Theological Society) meeting say that if he wanted to find out *what the Scripture does not mean,* he would consult the *Living Bible.*

Consider the vulgar and inappropriate language used: Gen 13:17, God tells Abraham to "hike in all directions;" 1 Sam 20:30, Saul reviling Jonathan, "You son of a bitch!;" 2 Sam 13:11, "Come to bed with me, my darling;" Isa 41:24, "Anyone who chooses you needs to have his head examined;" Zech 8:9, Jehovah says, "Get on with the job and finish it;" Matt 11:19, "You complain that I hang around with the worst sort of sinners;" Mark 2:16, "How can He stand it, to eat with such scum;" John 9:34, "You illegitimate bastard;" John 11:49, "You stupid idiots;" Acts 4:36, "Barny the Preacher."

The *Living Bible* has sold at least 40 million copies. In 1996 they released the *New Living Translation* which is not much of an improvement from the old one. See David Cloud, "The New Living Translation: A Weak Rendering of a Corrupt Text," *O Timothy* 13 (1996): 1–11.

New American Standard Bible

The NASB (1971) is another revision of the ASV, prepared by 32 scholars who believed in the inspiration of the Bible, and published by the Lockman Foundation. It is a literal translation of the Scriptures which sought to be "as close as possible to the actual wording and grammatical structure of the original writers." Although it has adopted a correct translational methodology, it failed in using a correct text. Dr Frank Logsdon who was one of the NASB translators, and who wrote the preface, later renounced the version he helped produce. He renounced all attachment to the NASB because it was based on the Westcott and Hort text. One may ask, "Well, didn't he know it in the first place?" Logsdon testified, "Well up to that time I thought the Westcott and Hort was the text. You were intelligent if you believed the Westcott and Hort. Some of the finest people in the world believe in that Greek text, the finest leaders that we have today. You'd be surprised; if I told you you wouldn't believe it. They haven't gone into it just as I hadn't gone into it; [they're] just taking it for granted. ... But I finally got to the place where I said, ... 'I'm in trouble, I can't refute these arguments; it's wrong; it's terribly wrong; it's frightfully wrong; and what am I going to do about it? ... I must under God renounce every attachment to the New American

Standard'" (See "From the NASV to the KJV," by S Franklin Logsdon. For a list of words/verses omitted in the NASB, see D K Madden, *A Critical Examination of the New American Standard Bible* [Australia: Privately printed, 1981].)

CHAPTER IX

A CRITICAL EVALUATION OF THE NEW INTERNATIONAL VERSION

The NIV (1978) is said to be the best-selling Bible version today. Many Christian bookshops in Singapore are well stocked with the NIV but not the KJV. To me, this is rather disturbing. Many are hoodwinked into thinking that the NIV is a good version. Although the NIV may be written in modern-day English, it is a dangerous version because it is based on an eclectic text with all its inherent corruptions, and on a dynamic equivalence method of translation.

This section seeks to expose the NIV for what it is: a version based on the corrupt Westcott-Hort text and theory, and a skewed translation methodology which renders not a literal, accurate translation but a subjective, opinionated interpretation of the Scriptures.

The NIV Is Based on a Corrupt Text

NIV Preface

According to the NIV preface, "The Greek text used in translating the New Testament was an eclectic one." NIV advocates deny that their version is based on the Westcott-Hort text. One local champion of the NIV said, "most if not all versions after the RSV are based on an eclectic text, and not on the UBS or Nestle-Aland text." This statement is inaccurate and incorrect.

UBSGNT and NANTG

The eclectic text is the United Bible Societies' Greek New Testament (UBSGNT), and the Nestle-Aland Greek New Testament (NANTG).

The UBSGNT acknowledges that its committee carried out its work "on the basis of Westcott and Hort's edition of the Greek New Testament" (4th ed, viii). The NANTG edition considered the TR to be the "poorest form of the New Testament Text" (so Westcott and Hort). Eberhard Nestle in an attempt to overthrow the traditional text based his critical text "on the editions of Tischendorf, Westcott-Hort, and Weymouth" (26th ed, 39). What level of influence did the Westcott-Hort text have on the NANTG edition? The "origin of the text itself was clearly traceable ... particularly in passages where the special theories of Westcott-Hort had dominant influence in its formation" (Ibid, 41). Although the NANTG renames itself as an "eclectic" text (Ibid, 42–3), the vestiges of WH remain; it is a stain difficult to remove. D K Madden wrote, "The translators of the New International Version state on page 8 of the Preface that they have used an eclectic (which according to the Oxford Dictionary implies borrowing freely from various sources) Greek text. This may be so, but an examination of their work clearly indicates that their choice of text has been greatly biased in favour of Nestle's Greek text which in turn is notorious for its adherence to the Westcott and Hort methods of textual criticism."

Radmacher and Hodges correctly pointed out that "The so-called 'new textus receptus'—the N/A and UBS editions—do not differ a whole lot from the text produced by Westcott-Hort in 1881" (Earl Radmacher and Zane C Hodges, *The NIV Reconsidered* [Dallas: Redencion Viva, 1990], 142–3). They also said, "The NIV as well as the NASB, NEB, JB, RSV, TEV, etc., simply adopt what is *today's* 'textus receptus'" which is "found in the two most widely printed editions of the Greek New Testament: the 26th edition of the Nestle/Aland text and the 3rd edition of the United Bible Societies text" (Ibid, 139).

Anderson and Anderson wrote, "twentieth century scholars have chosen, ... to abandon the Traditional Text in favour of a text based on these two Alexandrian manuscripts. The newest edition of this text is the United Bible Society's Third Edition. Although the New International Version translators were free to consider and incorporate readings from other Greek texts (thus rendering the basis of the New International Version New Testament an 'eclectic' text), it appears that they followed the United Bible Society's Third Edition for the New Testament work" (G W Anderson, and D E Anderson, *New International Version* [London: Trinitarian Bible Society, nd], 16).

What is the conclusion? Is the NIV based on Westcott and Hort? There were only three printed editions of the Greek New Testament that the NIV translators could use: (1) Textus Receptus (TR) published by the Trinitarian Bible Society which underlies the KJV, (2) UBSGNT, and (3) NANTG. Kenneth Barker, General editor of the NIV, said that the eclectic text is the UBSGNT and NANTG. NIV supporters who claim that the NIV is not based on Westcott and Hort are running from the facts.

The NIV Casts Doubt on God's Word

The Woman Taken in Adultery (John 7:53–8:11)

The story of the woman taken in adultery in John 7:53–8:11 is called the *pericope de adultera*. Modernistic scholars have attempted to remove this whole passage from the Bible. According to Westcott, "This account of a most characteristic incident in the Lord's life *is certainly not a part* of John's narrative." Not only has it been said that the *pericope de adultera* was not a part of John's Gospel, both Westcott and Hort insisted that the story "has *no right to a place* in the text of the four Gospels."

The Westcott-Hort based NIV has this misleading statement concerning the authenticity of John 7:53–8:11: "[The earliest and most reliable manuscripts and other ancient witnesses do not have John 7:53–8:11]." What are these so called "earliest" and "most reliable" manuscripts that do not have the *pericope de adultera*? They are Codex Vaticanus and Codex Sinaiticus, both fourth century manuscripts. Those who reject the *pericope de adultera* do so on a presuppositional bias that these two codices are superior manuscripts.

Are the above codices really reliable? One will do well to remember that these are the same 2 codices which attacked the doctrine of the Trinity by removing the *Johannine Comma* (1 John 5:7f). According to Dean Burgon, a godly and renowned Bible defender of the last century, the codices Vaticanus and Sinaiticus are among "the most corrupt copies in existence." Burgon wrote, "I am able to demonstrate that every one of them singly is in a high degree corrupt, and is condemned upon evidence older than itself" (for a full discussion, refer to John William Burgon's *The Revision Revised*). Although the above two codices may be "earliest" they are by no means "most reliable."

There is abundant evidence in support of the authenticity of the *pericope de adultera*. John 7:53–8:11 is found (1) in many Greek uncials and minuscules mainly of the Majority or Byzantine text-type, (2) in the ancient versions or translations: Old Latin, Vulgate, Syriac, Coptic, Armenian, and Ethiopic, and (3) in the writings of the Church Fathers: Didascalia, Ambrosiaster, Apostolic Constitutions, Ambrose, Jerome, and Augustine. Jerome (AD 340–420), the translator of the Latin Bible called the Vulgate, said this about the pericope de adultera: "… in the Gospel according to John in many manuscripts, both Greek and Latin, is found the story of the adulterous woman who was accused before the Lord."

Self-styled textual critics who arrogantly say: "This text has no place in Scripture; I will never preach from it!," should rather heed these wise words of Calvin: "it has always been received by the Latin Churches, and is found in many old Greek manuscripts, and contains nothing unworthy of an Apostolic Spirit, there is no reason why we should refuse to apply it to our advantage."

It must be noted that if John 7:53–8:11 is removed from the Gospel, it leaves a vacuum between the words "out of Galilee ariseth no prophet" (7:52), and "Then spake Jesus again unto them" (8:12). In 7:40–52, we find the private dialogue and debate among the Jewish populace, and between the temple servants and Pharisees over Jesus' identity; whether He was the Moses-like Prophet (Deut 18:15) or not. Jesus was out of the picture at that time. It is thus quite awkward to introduce Jesus so abruptly in 8:12 where it is recorded that He spoke to them "again." Jesus in verses 12–16 was teaching what is righteous judgment. The pericope de adultera provides the link between the two episodes. Jesus taught them "again" because He had already begun teaching the people before the scribes and Pharisees interrupted Him (8:2–3). Jesus' "light of the world" discourse clearly fits the context of the pericope de adultera. The Jewish religious leaders had failed to exercise righteous judgment because in condemning the adulteress, they failed to judge themselves for they were equally sinful (8:7–9). Jesus' judicial and yet merciful treatment of the adulteress clearly demonstrates that He alone as the light of the world is the true and perfect Judge (8:12).

The divinely inspired account of the woman taken in adultery rightfully belongs to the Gospel of John. Let us not hesitate to use it for our encouragement and comfort.

For further study, read John William Burgon, "The Woman Taken in Adultery: A Defense of the Authenticity of St John 7:53–8:11," in *Unholy Hands on the Bible*, ed Jay P Green (Lafayette: Sovereign Grace Trust Fund, 1990), F1–16; and Edward F Hills, *The King James Version Defended*, 150–9.

The Last 12 Verses of Mark (Mark 16:9–20)

Are the last 12 verses of Mark really Mark's? According to the NIV, "The most reliable early manuscripts and other ancient witnesses do not have Mark 16:9–20." Its Study Bible goes on to say, "serious doubt exists as to whether these verses belong to the Gospel of Mark. They are absent from important early manuscripts and display certain peculiarities of vocabulary, style and theological content that are unlike the rest of Mark. His Gospel probably ended at 16:8, ..." Here is another NIV attempt at scission. Practically every modern English version would insert this doubt over the authenticity of Mark 16:9–20. It is only the KJV which accepts it without question.

We affirm the authenticity of the last 12 verses of Mark together with Dean J W Burgon who wrote a scholarly 350-page defence of those celebrated verses. Burgon argued that the codices Sinaiticus and Vaticanus, which are said by many to be "most reliable," are actually "most corrupt." Burgon wrote, "Recent Editors of the New Testament insist that these 'last Twelve Verses' are not genuine. ... I am as convinced as I am of my life, that the reverse is the truth. ... I insist, on the contrary, that the Evidence relied on is untrustworthy,—untrustworthy in every particular. ... I am able to prove that this portion of the Gospel has been declared to be spurious on wholly mistaken grounds."

Furthermore, there is abundant manuscript evidence supporting the authenticity of Mark 16:9–20. E F Hills wrote, "They [Mark 16:9–20] are found in all the Greek manuscripts except *Aleph* [i.e. Sinaiticus], and B [i.e. Vaticanus], ... And more important, they were quoted as Scripture by early Church Fathers who lived one hundred and fifty years before *B* and *Aleph* were written, namely, Justin Martyr (c. 150), Tatian (c. 175), Irenaeus (c. 180), Hyppolytus (c. 200). Thus the earliest extant testimony is on the side of these last twelve verses."

How about the allegation that the last twelve verses are non-Marcan because of the difference in literary style? Metzger, for instance, argues against the last twelve verses because there are therein 17 words new to the Gospel of Mark. Such an argument is often fallacious because it wrongly assumes that an author has only one uniform style of writing. In any case, Burgon, after a careful comparison of Mark's first twelve verses with his last twelve verses, concluded, "It has been proved ... on the contrary, the style of S. Mark xvi. 9–20 is exceedingly like the style of S. Mark i. 9–20; and therefore, that *it is rendered probable by the Style* that the Author of the beginning of this Gospel was also the Author of the end of it. ... *these verses must needs be the work of S. Mark.*"

For further study, read John William Burgon, *The Last Twelve Verses of Mark* (Oxford, London: James Parker, 1871, reprinted in 1983 by The Bible For Today); D A Waite, *Dean John William Burgon's Vindication of the Last Twelve Verses of Mark* (Collingswood, NJ: The Bible For Today, 1994); Edward F Hills, *The King James Version Defended*, 159–68; and "The Authenticity of the Last Twelve Verses of the Gospel According to Mark," Article #106 (London: Trinitarian Bible Society, nd).

The NIV Scissors Out God's Word

According to Jack Moorman, there are a total of 140,521 Greek words in the traditional Greek New Testament. Now, out of these 140,521 words, 2,886 words are missing in the Critical Text of Nestle-Aland and Westcott and Hort. The amount of words scissored out is equivalent to the size of 1–2 John! See Jack A Moorman, *Modern Bibles: The Dark Secret* (California: Fundamental Evangelistic Association, nd). What are some of these words, verses and passages either omitted or questioned (based on UBSGNT cf NIV)?

Entire Passages Questioned

The NIV questions the authenticity of Mark 16:9–20 and John 7:53–8:11 with such comments, "[The *most reliable early* manuscripts and other ancient witnesses do not have Mark 16:9–20.]," and "[The *earliest and most reliable* manuscripts and other ancient witnesses do not have John 7:53–8:11.]"

Entire Verses Omitted

The NIV omits the following 17 verses in their entirety: Matt 17:21, 18:11, 23:14; Mark 7:16, 9:44,46, 11:26; 15:28; Luke 17:36, 23:17; John 5:4; Acts 8:37, 15:34, 24:7, 28:29; Rom 16:24; 1 John 5:7.

Portions of Verses Omitted or Modified

The following verses contain partial omissions or modifications:

In Matthew

"without a cause" (5:22), "by them of old time" (5:27), "For thine is the kingdom and the power and the glory forever. Amen" (6:13), "to repentance" (9:13), "among the people" (9:35), "Lebbaeus, whose surname was" (10:3), "raise the dead" (10:8), "of the heart" (12:35), "Jesus saith unto them" (13:51), "draweth nigh unto me with their mouth" (15:8), "at his feet" (18:29), "from my youth" (19:20), "and whatsoever is right, that shall ye receive" (20:7), "For many be called, but few chosen" (20:16), "and to be baptized with the baptism that I am baptized with" (2x in 20:22,23), "take him away, and" (22:13), "observe" (23:3), "wherein the Son of Man cometh" (25:13), "false witnesses" (26:60b), "that it might be fulfilled which was spoken by the prophet: They parted my garments among them, and upon my vesture did they cast lots" (27:35).

In Mark

"Isaiah the prophet" (1:2), "of the kingdom" (1:14), "to repentance" (2:17), "whole as the other" (3:5), "to heal sicknesses and" (3:15), "of the air" (4:4), "Verily, I say unto you, It shall be more tolerable for Sodom and Gomorrha in the day of judgment than for that city" (6:11), "bread, for they have nothing to eat" (6:36), "they found fault" (7:2), "and fasting" (9:29), "into the fire that never shall be quenched" (9:45), "and every sacrifice shall be salted with salt" (9:49), "for them that trust in riches" (10:24), "in the name of the Lord" (11:10), "and at him they cast stones" (12:4), "This is the first commandment" (12:30), "with all the soul" (12:33), "spoken of by Daniel the prophet" (13:14), "And another said, Is it I?" (14:19), "because of me this night" (14:27), "and thy speech agreeth thereto" (14:70).

In Luke

"blessed art thou among women" (1:28), "when she saw him" (1:29), "hath visited" (1:78), "but by every word of God" (4:4), "Get thee behind me, Satan" (4:8), "to heal the brokenhearted" (4:18), "Christ" (4:41), "and both are preserved" (5:38), "whole as the other" (6:10), "treasure of his heart" (6:45), "that had been sick" (7:10), "And the Lord said" (7:31), "and they that were with him" (8:45), "and sayest thou, Who touched me?" (8:45), "and he put them all out" (8:54), "even as Elias did" (9:54), "and said, Ye know not what manner of spirit ye are of" (9:55), "For the Son of man is not come to destroy men's lives, but to save them" (9:56). "when he departed" (10:35), "Thy will be done, as in heaven, so in earth" (11:2), "but deliver us from evil" (11:4), "bread of any of you that is a father, will he give him a stone? or if he ask" (11:11), "the prophet" (11:29), "scribes and Pharisees, hypocrites" (11:44), "that they might accuse him" (11:54), "against thee" (17:3), "him? I trow not" (17:9), "and saw him" (19:5), "Why tempt ye me?" (20:23), "took her to wife, and he died childless" (20:30), "in my kingdom" (22:30), "And the Lord said" (22:31), "struck him on the face and" (22:64), "me, nor let me go" (22:68), "and of the chief priests" (23:23), written over him in letters of Greek, and Latin, and Hebrew" (23:38), "and certain others with them" (24:1), "and of an honeycomb" (24:42).

In John

"which is in heaven" (3:13), "not perish, but" (3:15), "the Christ" (4:42), "waiting for the moving of the water" (5:3), "and sought to slay him" (5:16), "to the disciples, and the disciples" (6:11), "whereinto his disciples were entered" (6:22), "on me" (6:47), "being convicted by their own conscience" (8:9), "and saw none but the woman" (8:10), "through the midst of them, and so passed by" (8:59), "the pool of" (9:11), "as I said unto you" (10:26), "from the place where the dead was laid" (11:41), "which had been dead" (12:1), "in the world" (17:12), "and led him away" (19:16).

In Acts

"ye have taken" (2:23), "of the Lord" (7:30), "him shall ye hear" (7:37), "it is hard for thee to kick against the pricks" (9:5), "he shall tell thee what thou oughtest to do" (10:6), "which were sent unto him from Cornelius" (10:21), "who, when he cometh, shall speak unto thee" (10:32), "Ye must be circumcised, and keep the law" (15:24), "which believed not" (17:5), "I must by all means keep this feast that cometh in Jerusalem" (18:21), "that were of Paul's company" (21:8), "that they observe no such thing, save only" (21:25), "and were afraid" (22:9), "unto his death" (22:20), "and would have judged according to our law" (24:6), "commanding his accusers to come unto thee" (24:8), "of the dead" (24:15), "that he might loose him" (24:26).

In Romans

"of Christ" (1:16), "and upon all" (3:22), "who walk not after the flesh, but after the Spirit" (8:1), "for us" (8:26), "of righteousness" (9:31), "of the law" (9:32), "preach the gospel of peace" (10:15), "But if it be of works, then is it no more grace: otherwise work is no more work" (11:6), "and he that regardeth not the day, to the Lord he doth not regard it. He that eateth, eateth to the Lord, for he giveth God thanks; and he that eateth not, to the Lord he eateth not, and giveth God thanks" (14:6), "or is offended, or is made weak" (14:21), "I will come to you" (15:24), "of the gospel" (15:29).

In 1 Corinthians

"for us" (5:7), "and in your spirit, which are God's" (6:20), "of Christ" (9:18), "for me" (10:23), "for the earth is the Lord's, and the fulness thereof" (10:28), "Take, eat" (11:24), "unworthily" (11:29), "the Lord" (15:47).

In 2 Corinthians

"that we would receive" (8:4), "in glorying" (12:11), "I write" (13:2).

In Galatians

"that ye should not obey the truth" (3:1), "in Christ" (3:17), "through Christ" (4:7).

In Ephesians

"by Jesus Christ" (3:9), "of our Lord Jesus Christ" (3:14), "other" (4:17), "of his flesh, and of his bones" (5:30). In Philippians "rule, let us mind the same things" (3:16).

In Colossians

"and the Lord Jesus Christ" (1:2), "through his blood" (1:14), "and of the Father and" (2:2), "of the sins" (2:11).

In 1 Thessalonians

"from God our Father and the Lord Jesus Christ" (1:1).

In 2 Thessalonians

"as God" (2:4).

In 1 Timothy

"in Christ" (2:7), "not greedy of filthy lucre" (3:3), "who" instead of "God" (3:16), "in spirit" (4:12), "good and" (5:4), "man or" (5:16), "from such withdraw thyself" (6:5), "and it is certain" (6:7).

In 2 Timothy

"of the Gentiles" (1:11).

In Hebrews

"by himself" (1:3), "and didst set him over the works of thy hands" (2:7), "firm unto the end" (3:6), "and their sins" (8:12), "O God" (10:9), "saith the Lord" (10:30), "was delivered of a child" (11:11), "were persuaded of them" (11:13), "or thrust through with a dart" (12:20). In James "adulterers and" (4:4).

In 1 Peter

"through the Spirit" (1:22), "for us" (4:1), "on their part he is evil spoken of, but on your part he is glorified" (4:14).

In 1 John

"from the beginning" (2:7), "Christ is come in the flesh" (4:3), "in heaven: the Father, the Word, and the Holy Spirit; and these three are one" (5:7), "and that ye may believe on the name of the Son of God" (5:13).

In Revelation

"the beginning and the ending" (1:8), "I am Alpha and Omega, the first and the last: and" (1:11), "which are in Asia" (1:11), "him that liveth for ever and ever" (5:14), "and the angel stood" (11:1), "and art to come" (11:17), "here are they" (14:12), "over his mark" (15:2), "O Lord" (16:5), "another out of" (16:7), "of the earth and" (16:14), "the Lord" (19:1), "of them which are saved" (21:24).

The Johannine Comma Removed (1 John 5:7–8)

Is there a clear biblical proof text for the doctrine of the Trinity? 1 John 5:7–8 in the KJV reads, "For there are three that bear record <u>in heaven, the Father, the Word, and the Holy Ghost: and these three are</u>

one. And there are three that bear witness in earth, the spirit, and the water, and the blood: and these three agree in one." The words underlined constitute the Johannine Comma (Gk: *koptein*, "to cut off"). The Comma proves the doctrine of the Holy Trinity—that "There are three persons in the Godhead: the Father, the Son, and the Holy Ghost; and these three are one God, the same in substance, equal in power, and glory" (WSC Q 6).

Why is this verse so seldom used to teach the doctrine of the Holy Trinity? The oft-quoted NT texts for the Trinity are Matt 3:16–17, 28:19, 2 Cor 13:14, and Rev 4:8, but why not 1 John 5:7f? One will reply, "How can I when my Bible does not have it?" Therein lies the problem; with 1 John 5:7f missing in so many of the modern Bible versions like the NIV, RSV, and NASB, it is no wonder that many Christians are ignorant of this verse. And even if they do know that this verse exists, they hesitate to use it because they have been deceived into thinking that it is not part of God's Word. *The NIV Study Bible*, for instance, says that 1 John 5:7f "is not found in any Greek manuscript or NT translation prior to the 16th century." On account of this they argue that 1 John 5:7f is spurious. It is unfortunate that even *The King James Study Bible* (Thomas Nelson Publishers) doubted the authenticity of this verse.

It is not true that 1 John 5:7f is absent in all pre-16th century Greek manuscripts and NT translations. The text is found in eight extant Greek manuscripts, and at least five of them are dated before the 16th century. Furthermore, there is abundant support for 1 John 5:7f from the Latin translations. There are at least 8,000 extant Latin manuscripts, and many of them contain 1 John 5:7f; the really important ones being the Old Latin which Church Fathers like Tertullian (AD 155–220), and Cyprian (AD 200–258) used. Now, out of the very few Old Latin manuscripts with the fifth chapter of 1 John, at least four of them contain the Comma. Since these Latin versions were derived from the Greek NT, there is reason to believe that 1 John 5:7f has very early Greek attestation, hitherto lost. There is also reason to believe that Jerome's Latin Vulgate (AD 340–420), which has the Johannine Comma, was translated from an untampered Greek text he had in his possession, and that he regarded the Comma to be a genuine part of 1 John. Jerome in his *Prologue to the Canonical Epistles* wrote, "irresponsible translators left out this testimony [i.e., 1 John 5:7f] in the Greek codices." Edward F Hills concluded, "... it was not trickery that was responsible for the inclusion of the Johannine Comma in the Textus Receptus, but the usage of the Latin speaking Church."

This leads us to the so-called "promise" of Erasmus. Westcott and Hort advocate—Bruce Metzger—made this claim which became the popular argument against the Johannine Comma. He wrote, "Erasmus promised that he would insert *the Comma Johanneum*, as it is called, in future editions if a single Greek manuscript could be found that contained the passage. At length such a copy was found—or made to order." This view against the authenticity of 1 John 5:7f is parroted by anti-KJVists Stewart Custer, D A Carson and James R White. Is this truly what happened? H J de Jonge of the faculty of theology, Leiden University, an authority on Erasmus, says that Metzger's view on Erasmus' promise "has no foundation in Erasmus' work. Consequently it is highly improbable that he included the difficult passage because he considered himself bound by any such promise." Yale professor—Roland Bainton— another Erasmian expert agrees with de Jonge furnishing proof from Erasmus' own writing that Erasmus' inclusion of 1 John 5:7f was not due to a so-called "promise" but the fact that he believed "the verse was in the Vulgate and must therefore have been in the Greek text used by Jerome." The Erasmian "promise" is thus a myth!

It has been suggested that the Johannine Comma did not come from the Apostle John himself but from an unknown person who invented and inserted it into 1 John 5 so that Christianity would have a clear Trinitarian proof text. Up till this point in time, no one is able to identify this mysterious person who tried to "help" the Church. He is probably a fictitious character. In any case, it is highly unlikely that 1 John 5:7f is the work of a well-meaning interpolator. When we look at the text itself, the phrase, "the Father, *the Word*, and the Holy Spirit," naturally reflects Johannine authorship (cf John 1:1,14). An interpolator would rather have used the more familiar and perhaps stronger Trinitarian formula—"the Father, *the Son*, and the Holy Spirit." "The Word" or "The *Logos*" of 1 John 5:7f surely points to the Apostle John as its source for it is distinctively John who uses the term "the Word" to mean "Christ" in all his writings.

There is nothing in the Johannine Comma that goes against the fundamentals of the Christian faith. It is thoroughly biblical, and theologically accurate in its Trinitarian statement. There is really no good reason why we should not regard it as authentic, and employ it as the clearest proof-text in the Scripture for the doctrine of the Holy Trinity.

Serious students will want to look up these two seminal monographs: (1) Edward F Hills, *The King James Version Defended*, 209–13; and (2) Michael Maynard, *A History of the Debate Over 1 John 5:7–8* (Tempe: Comma Publications, 1995). The latter, by a librarian, in defence of the Johannine Comma is especially thorough and helpful. The onus is now on KJV detractors to address the documents, evidences, and arguments garnered by Maynard.

It is no coincidence that the above missing verses are also missing in the UBSGNT and NANTG. Coincidence? Peter Eng—a local NIV-champion—in an attempt to refute this author wrote, "I am amazed that Jeffrey Khoo is so ignorant as to say modern versions are based on the WH Theory. He should know that most if not all versions after the RSV are based on an eclectic text, and not on the UBS or Nestle-Aland text." My rejoinder: "If the NIV is not based on the UBS or NA Greek text, then 'I am amazed' over the striking similarities between those Greek texts and the NIV in omitting the exact same verses of NT Scripture!" James R White himself, the most recent opponent of the KJV-only position, would largely agree with me, "There are two main modern texts, the United Bible Societies 4th Edition, and the Nestle-Aland 27th edition, both of which have the same text but differ in other matters such as punctuation, textual apparatus, etc. These texts are more 'Alexandrian' in character than the *Textus Receptus*, which was based upon Byzantine manuscripts, but *less* Alexandrian than the text produced by Westcott and Hort in 1881" (*The King James Only Controversy* [Minneapolis: Bethany House Publishers, 1995], 45). It must be said that although the modern critical Greek NTs are "less Alexandrian" they are still *very* Alexandrian by the amount of verses removed and passages questioned as we have discussed earlier and shall see later.

The NIV Attacks Vital Doctrines of the Christian Faith

Attack on the Eternal Generation of God the Son

The eternal generation of the second person of the Holy Trinity (i.e. Jesus is the eternally begotten Son of God) is an important doctrine of the Christian Faith. The fourth century Athanasian and Nicene Creeds state that Jesus is both Son and God *"only-begotten, ... of the Father before all the ages."* The 17th century Westminster Confession likewise followed the ancient creeds in describing the relationship that exists within the Godhead: "In the unity of the Godhead, there be three persons, of one substance, power and eternity; God the Father, God the Son, and God the Holy Ghost. The Father is of none, neither begotten nor proceeding; the Son is *eternally begotten* of the Father; the Holy Ghost eternally proceeding from the Father and the Son" (II.III).

All three ancient creeds describe Christ as only begotten or eternally begotten. Every doctrine must be based on the Bible. Where in the Bible is Jesus being described as the only begotten Son of God? If you have the KJV you will find it in John 1:14, 18; 3:16, 18; and 1 John 4:9. But if you are using the NIV, you will have a hard time finding this doctrine in the Bible. The term "only begotten" with reference to Christ has been conveniently removed by the NIV. It mistranslates the Greek *monogenes* as "one and only." Problem is *monogenes* does not just mean "one and only." The Greek *monogenes* comes from 2 words: *monos* meaning "only" and *gennao* meaning "to beget" or "to generate." The KJV translates it literally and accurately as "only begotten." The NIV, on the other hand, by deleting the word "begotten" has erased this important doctrine on the person of Christ from the Scriptures. It has subtracted from God's Word; a very dangerous thing to do (Rev 22:19). It cannot be trusted.

Attack on the Virgin Birth of Christ

In Luke 2:33 we read, "And *Joseph and his mother* marvelled at those things which were spoken of him" (KJV). In the NIV, it is like this, *"The child's father and mother* marveled at what was said about him." Do you see the problem here with the NIV? The NIV makes Joseph the father of Jesus! The NIV rendering of this verse is totally out of line for the following reasons: (1) the word "child" is not in the traditional Greek text, (2) the word "father" is not in the Greek text, (2) the possessive pronoun

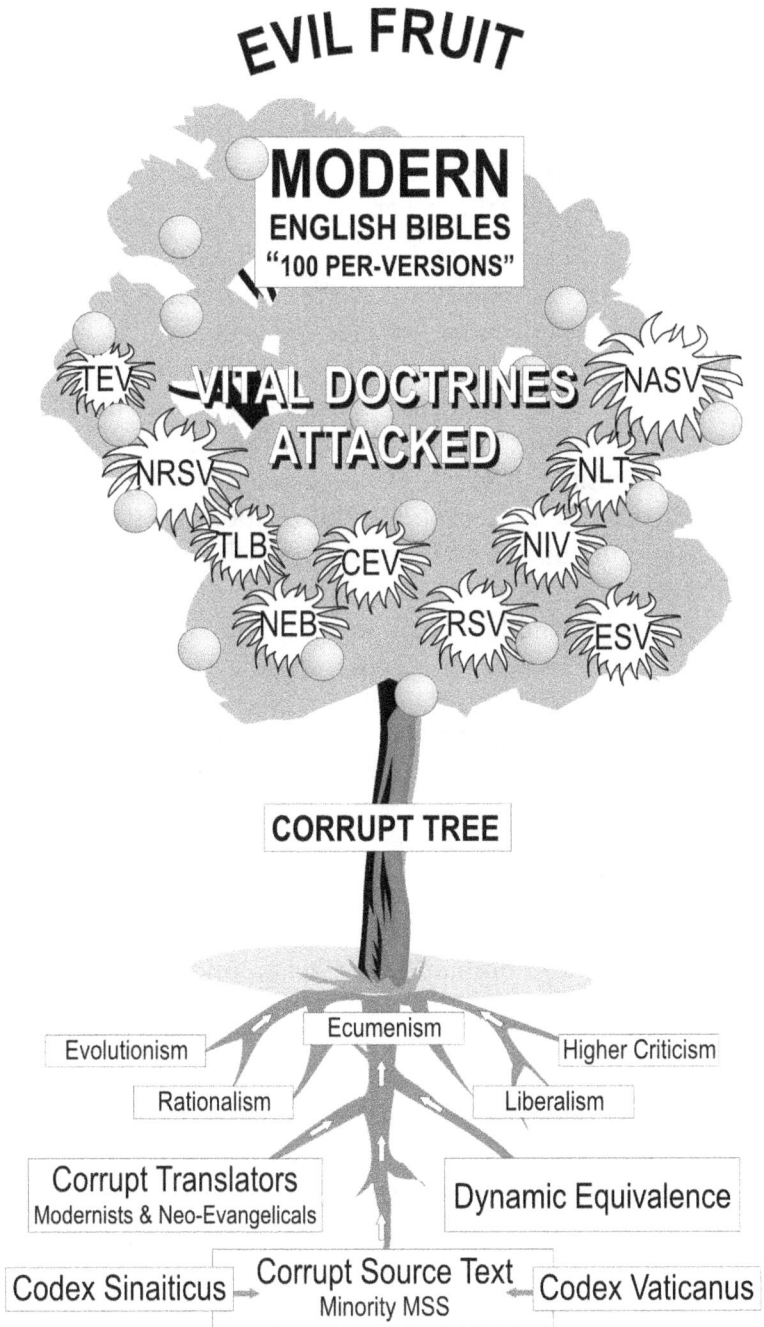

EVIL FRUIT

MODERN
ENGLISH BIBLES
"100 PER-VERSIONS"

VITAL DOCTRINES ATTACKED

TEV NASV
NRSV NLT
TLB CEV NIV
NEB RSV ESV

CORRUPT TREE

Ecumenism

Evolutionism Higher Criticism

Rationalism Liberalism

Corrupt Translators
Modernists & Neo-Evangelicals

Dynamic Equivalence

Codex Sinaiticus → Corrupt Source Text
Minority MSS ← Codex Vaticanus

". . . a corrupt tree bringeth forth evil fruit."

"his" is connected to Mary alone (*he meter autou*), and does not include Joseph. Those who do not know better would probably come to the conclusion that Joseph was the direct, natural father of Jesus. The NIV has caused Luke to contradict the virgin birth. Jesus has only one Father, and that is the First Person of the Holy Trinity. Joseph was neither physically nor spiritually the father of Jesus.

However, NIV advocates will point out verse 41 which called Joseph and Mary "his parents" (so KJV as in NIV). The fact that Joseph and Mary were indeed parents of Jesus—Joseph being legally a "parent" and not naturally the "father" of Jesus—would prove the point that the biblical writers were careful not to attribute the title "father" to Joseph, for Jesus only has one Father, and that is His Father in Heaven—the First Person of the Holy Trinity. In verse 43, we again see the inspired writers carefully distinguishing Joseph's actual relationship with Jesus by the words "Joseph and his mother," again purposely avoiding calling Joseph Jesus' "father." Jesus Himself refused calling Joseph his "father," and gently corrected his mother when she said, "thy father and I have sought thee" which drew this response from the Lord, "How is it that ye sought me? wist ye not that I must be about my *Father's* business?" Why did not Jesus use "God," or "the Lord," but "Father" at this juncture? I believe it is to correct any misconception that Joseph was in any way His father. God alone was His Father.

Attack on the Theanthropic Person of Christ

1 Tim 3:16 has to be one of the clearest texts of Scripture proving the full deity and full humanity of Christ, "And without controversy great is the mystery of godliness: *God was manifest in the flesh*, ..." But if you had the NIV, you would have a difficult time proving this. Instead of the reading, "God was manifest in the flesh," you have "He appeared in a body." The NIV obscures (1) the deity of Christ by removing "God" and replacing it with just "He," and (2) the humanity of Christ by replacing " the flesh," with "a body" (a body may not necessarily be of "flesh and blood"). The word in the original is *sarx* meaning "flesh," not *soma* meaning "body." It is also interesting and significant to note that the KJV translators never rendered *sarx* as body and *soma* as flesh (see Lau Yeong Shoon, *A Textus Receptus-King James Version Greek-English Lexicon of the New Testament*, MDiv thesis, Far Eastern Bible College, 1997, 214,

228). The KJV recognised the proper distinctions between the two; something the NIV translators obviously failed to do in their dynamic-equivalence blindness.

Why does the NIV translate 1 Tim 3:16 as "He" and not "God?" It is simply because they chose to adopt a Westcott-Hort reading of the text. According to Westcott and Hort, since the Sinai and Vatican codices read "he who," instead of "God," it must be the correct reading. And mind you, this is over against *the majority* of the Greek manuscripts including certain Alexandrian ones which read *Theos*, "God," instead of *hos*, "he who." Many modern versions like the NIV happily follow Westcott and Hort in corrupting the Word of God. How can NIV defenders deny that the NIV is based on Westcott and Hort? How can NIV users who say they love God's Word continue to use a version which supports the unbelieving views of those two enemies of Christ? For more discussion on this verse, see "God was Manifest in the Flesh (1 Tim 3:16)," Article #103 (London, Trinitarian Bible Society, nd).

Attack on the Eternal Punishment of Sinners in Hell

The NIV has a habit of removing words that are not easily understood by the modern reader. In so doing, proof texts for certain important doctrines have also been removed. One example is the Hebrew word *sheol* where the KJV sometimes translates as "the grave," and other times as "hell." The NIV removes the concept of "hell" (i.e. a place of eternal punishment) when it refuses to translate *sheol* as hell. Thus, in Ps 9:17, "the wicked shall be turned into hell" is changed to "the wicked return to the grave." Even Lucifer (i.e. Satan) will not be "brought down to hell," but "brought down to the grave" (Isa 14:15). By never translating *sheol* as hell, the NIV has effectively made our Bible poorer on the teaching of eternal punishment. It is no surprise that today more and more Christians are rejecting the traditional doctrine that there is a place of eternal conscious torment called hell where all reprobates will finally be consigned. So-called evangelicals like Clark Pinnock and John Stott are nowadays espousing the annihilation doctrine of the Jehovah's Witnesses. Did they influence the NIV, or did the NIV influence them?

Attack on Christ as the Judge Who Is God

In Rom 14:10,12 we are told, "we shall all stand before the judgment seat of *Christ*. ... So then every one of us shall give account of himself to *God*." In the NIV, the deity of Christ is denied. It reads, "For we will all stand before *God's* judgment seat ... so then, each of us will give an account of himself to God." In the KJV, all men are to stand before Christ, giving account to God. The equation is clear: Christ is God. But the NIV changes "Christ" in verse 10 to "God," and by so doing, renders verse 12 a simple restatement of verse 10, without affirming the deity of Christ.

Anderson and Anderson correctly comment, "Here a wonderful verse which plainly declares our Saviour's deity is done away with without the average Christian even knowing it. The deity of Christ is attested in this passage in some Alexandrian manuscripts, the majority of other manuscripts, many ancient versions, and at least ten church fathers. It is missing from only a handful of manuscripts (seven), which unfortunately for the church includes the two considered to the best by modern scholars: the Vatican manuscript and ... the Sinai manuscript. The New International Version, by this omission, does more than delete a few words; it reflects the high handed approach to textual criticism threatening the Church today" ("New International Version," 18).

The NIV Mistranslates God's Word

Mistranslation of Psalm 12:7 on the Preservation of God's Word

The NIV reads, "And the words of the LORD are flawless like silver refined in a furnace of clay, purified seven times. O LORD, you will keep us safe and protect us from such people forever" (Ps 12:6–7). Note the change from "keep them" to "keep us," and "preserve them" to "protect us." They changed the pronouns from third plural (i.e. "them") to first plural (i.e. "us"). Is this a correct or accurate translation?

In Hebrew, the first word is *tishmerem*. The *-em* suffix means "them" not "us." He will keep "them" (so KJV) is correct. The second word is *titzrennu*. The *-ennu* suffix (with an energetic nun) is third singular (i.e. "him"), not first plural (i.e. "us"). The energetic nun is emphatic (i.e. "every one of them"). So it should be translated preserve "them" (i.e. "every *single word of His words*") not "us" (i.e. "every *single person of His people*"). By incorrectly and inaccurately translating Ps 12:7, the NIV has effectively removed the doctrine of Bible preservation from this text. For an excellent study of the doctrine of Bible preservation in the light of Ps 12, see Shin Yeong Gil, "God's Promise to Preserve His Word: An Exegetical Study of Psalm 12:5–7," ThM thesis, Far Eastern Bible College, 1999, published in *The Burning Bush* 6 (2000): 150–182.

Mistranslation of Isaiah 49:12 on God's Promise to the Chinese

(Timothy Tow, "NIV Turns 'Land of Sinim' into 'Region of Aswan' by a Twist of the Ball-Pen!" *The Burning Bush* 2 [1996]: 73–5)

"The translation of KJV of Isaiah 49:12, 'Behold, these shall come from far: and, lo, these from the north and from the west; and these <u>from the land of Sinim</u>' from the Hebrew text is correct. How does the NIV differ to translate 'from the land of Sinim' into 'from the region of Aswan'?

"The word 'Sinim' in Hebrew is סִינִים. And the word for 'Aswan' according to the NIV in Ezekiel 29:10 and 30:6 is סְוֵנֵה. Now סִינִים is pronounced 'Sinim' but סְוֵנֵה which is pronounced 'Seveneh' is translated 'Aswan'. But why is *Sinim* at Isaiah 49:12 by a twist of the NIV's ball-pen also become 'Aswan'? Even the non-Hebrew reader can see that *Sinim* and Aswan are two different words. Perhaps the NIV translators think they can palm off their ware to the unwary non-Hebrew English reader.

"Another difference between the KJV and NIV translations is the NIV rendering of 'land' into 'region' whereas *'eretz* has almost always been translated 'land', 'earth', or 'ground'. Now if the NIV translates 'the *land* of Zebulon and the *land* of Naphtali' from the word *'eretz* (Isa 9:1) and Zebulon and Naphtali are small tribes, why does not NIV use the word 'region' here? The right word for 'region' in Hebrew is *chebel* according to the Hebrew lexicon (BDB, 286). There is no valid reason to translate *'eretz* as 'region' except for the sinister purpose of demoting the Land of Sinim into some Egyptian outback.

"The land of Sinim, according to Hastings' *Dictionary of the Bible*, from the context, must have been the extreme south or east of the known world (*Dictionary of the Bible*, ed James Hastings, sv 'Sinim'). The LXX favours the view that a country in the east is intended, and some modern commentators have identified Sinim with China, the land of the

Sinae. The ancients' view that Sinim refers to China is attested overwhelmingly by continuing modern Hebrew usage. My English-Hebrew, Hebrew-English lexicon by Prof M Segal and Prof M B Dagut, says China is סין (Sin) and Chinese is סיני (*English-Hebrew Dictionary*, sv 'China', 'Chinese'). The root of 'Sinim' is 'Sin,' so 'Sinim' points most assuredly to China and not to Aswan, which is translated from a different word סונה as stated above. Thus, one who is well-versed in Chinese is called a sinologue and sinology is the study of Chinese language, history, customs, etc; and the war between China and Japan was called the Sino-Japanese war.

"Let me quote from Dr Allan A MacRae my teacher on the above subject under discussion. In his *Studies in Isaiah*, Dr MacRae says as a matter of fact: 'In verse 12 the remarkable extent of the work of the servant is clearly indicated with people coming to his light from the north and from the west and even from the land of Sinim (China). What a marvelous prediction of the extension of the gospel of deliverance from sin through the servant of the Lord to the very ends of the world! How wonderfully it has been fulfilled in these days when groups of believers have come to the Savior from so many sections of the earth, even including this very land of China, which must have seemed in the days of Isaiah to be the utmost fringe of civilization. Truly He has become 'a light to the Gentiles'.' [Allan A MacRae, *Studies in Isaiah* (Hatfield PA: Interdisciplinary Biblical Research Institute, 1995), 237; Edward J Young wrote likewise, 'In any attempt to identify the land of Sinim we must look for a place far from Palestine. An ancient interpretation would identify it with China, ...' (*The Book of Isaiah*, NICOT [Grand Rapids: Wm B Eerdmans Publishing Co, 1972], 3:282, 294).]

"Furthermore, let us see how the translators of the Chinese Bible treat the Hebrew text. They translate the land of Sinim as *Chin Kuo* the Kingdom or Country of Chin, and 'Chin' is a root word for China, verily, as it was <u>Chin</u> Shih Hwang Ti the first Emperor who united the many ancient states into one China. This is a good translation in the tradition of the LXX, and in line with time-honoured Hebrew usage to this day.

"Speaking from my experience as a Certified Chinese Interpreter of the Supreme Court, Singapore in my young days, whenever there was any doubt in the translation of a Chinese document into English, the Judge would know exactly and objectively what the original says, and not some dynamic equivalent, the subjective NIV style. The KJV renders the Hebrew and Greek of the Bible without subtraction or addition, least by juggling, when מאָרֶץ סִינִים ('from the land of Sinim') can be twisted to read 'from the region of Aswan.' Let us have an answer from the learned NIV translators."

Mistranslation of 2 Thessalonians 3:6 on Secondary Separation
(Charles Seet, "The Principle of Secondary Separation [2 Thess 3:6–15],"
The Burning Bush 2 [1996]: 41–2)

"Paul wrote this passage because some in the church refused to work. But the scope of the sin is not limited to slothfulness. The loafers are referred to in 3:6 as 'every brother walking disorderly.' Why did the apostle choose to use this unspecific phrase rather than something more convenient, like 'everyone who is not working'? The word *ataktōs* is a *hapax legomenon* (i.e. a word occuring only once in the scriptures) and is the adverbial form of the word *ataktos*, which itself occurs in 1 Thess 5:14, and is also a *hapax legomenon*. The verb form, *atakteō*, occurs significantly in the same context (in v.7) as the adverb, and it also is a *hapax legomenon*. It therefore becomes difficult to attach any meaning more specific than what is known from the common usage of this word ('not in proper order', as found in 3 Macc 1:19; Philo, Josephus, Bel and the Dragon, etc.).

"Therefore the word 'disorderly' used in 2 Thess 3:6 need not necessarily be referring only to people who are not working. Unfortunately, English translations like the NIV have paraphrased the Greek in rendering the passage: *We command you, brothers, to keep away from every brother who is idle...* This obscures the principle and limits the passage to only one *application* of the principle, namely—the problem of loafers.

"After using this phrase, the apostle Paul goes on to use another equally non-specific phrase: 'not according to the tradition which they received from us.' The word at issue here is *tradition* (*paradosis*). This word is found only five times in Paul's epistles (1 Cor 11:2, Gal 1:14, Col 2:8) and twice in 2 Thessalonians: here, and in 2:15. In none of these other occurrences, is the word ever employed in the sense of one particular teaching or commandment alone. It stands for all Christian teaching, oral or written.

"Since both of these non-specific phrases are found in the very first verse of the paragraph in which Paul proceeds to address the issue of errant non-working brethren, it would not be unreasonable to conclude that he deliberately chose to begin his instruction by stating a general principle, before dealing specifically with the problem itself. This pattern can be demonstrated in many other Pauline passages (Rom 13:1,6; 1 Cor 6:12,13–20; Gal 5:1ff). The whole of v.6, is therefore *a general principle*, that believers ought to separate themselves from every one in their midst who was deliberately disobeying any part of the whole body of inspired instruction. Thus, the main issue this paragraph addresses is *disobedience*."

The NIV Opposes a Strictly Messianic Fulfilment of Isaiah 7:14 in Its Study Bible

Jesus Christ was the only one who fulfilled the precious virgin birth prophecy of Isa 7:14. The NIV however suggests otherwise by rendering *ha 'almah* in Isa 7:14 as "the virgin" instead of "a virgin" (KJV). Radmacher and Hodges rightly criticised the NIV's treatment of Isa 7:14. According to them, "with the use of the definite article 'the' with 'virgin,' the NIV has laid the groundwork for a quasi-liberal view of Isaiah 7:14.

"This becomes obvious when we read *The NIV Study Bible* note. The note states: '7:14 *sign*. A sign was normally fulfilled within a few years (see 20:3; 37:30; cf. 8:18).' This statement leads to the legitimate inference that we should not look for a distant (that is, *Messianic*) fulfillment of 7:14 during the New Testament period! The flawed NIV view of Messianic prophecy is once again in evidence.

"The note continues: '*virgin*. May refer to a young woman betrothed to Isaiah (8:3), who was to become his second wife (his first wife presumably having died after Shear-jashub was born). In Gen. 24:43 the same Hebrew word (*'almah*) refers to a woman about to be married (see also Pr. 30:19). Mt. 1:23 apparently understood the woman mentioned here to be a type (foreshadowing) of the Virgin Mary.' So now the cat is out of the bag! In the NIV, '*the virgin*' apparently is intended to refer to a specific individual who, though not previously named, is very much a part of the larger context of this announcement. To put it briefly, '*the virgin*' refers to '*the woman*' Isaiah is about to marry. Only if the prediction is viewed typologically, so we are told, can we find any validity to Matthew's use of this text in reference to the Virgin Mary.

"Despite the finely honed statements of the NIV study note, what the note really means is this: Isaiah 7:14 is not a direct prophecy about the virgin birth at all. Indeed, the woman to whom it *did* really apply gave birth in a perfectly normal way! But nobody could deduce such a conclusion from Matthew's use of the text. Haven't we been through all this before? What about the long-running debate in the 19th and early 20th centuries, between liberals and conservatives, over whether Isaiah 7:14 truly predicts the virgin birth or not? Is not the Christian public ready for an evangelical translation that concedes the basic case to liberal theology and then clings to the slender reed of typology to preserve its weakened conservative credentials? We hope not.

"Let this be said clearly. The authors of this book hold firmly to the traditional evangelical view that Isaiah 7:14 directly predicts the virgin birth of our Lord. No other reading of this text comports with the inspired use of it made by Matthew" (*The NIV Reconsidered*, 52–4). See also my article, "The Sign of the Virgin Birth," *The Burning Bush* 1 (1995): 5–33.

WHAT IS YOUR PERSUASION?

TWO STREAMS OF ENGLISH BIBLES		
	King James Bible	**Modern Versions**
1. THRUST	Spirit of 16th Century Reformation	Spirit of Romish Reformation
2. TEXT (MSS)	Preserved & Faithful "Traditional Text" Textus Receptus (TR) nearest to original	Corrupt & Perverted "Minority Text" Vatican & Sinai MSS "among the worst" —Burgon
3. TRANSLATORS (MEN)	Only faithful, godly men with "high view" of Scripture	Mixed group including liberals, heretics, apostates, enemies of God's Word
4. TECHNIQUE (METHODOLOGY)	"Verbal Equivalence" Word for word, faithful transmission of God's words	"Dynamic Equivalence" Men's thoughts in place of God's words
5. TRANSLATION	Protestant Bible — KJV, AV (1611) Vital doctrines and authority of God's Word fully preserved	Mixed multitude — ecumenical versions Vital doctrines attacked, authority of God's Word undermined
QUESTION: Which is God's Word? You judge.		

CHAPTER X

THE SUPERIORITY OF THE KING JAMES VERSION

The KJV Is Superior because It Is Based on the Preserved Text

All Christians should believe in the inspiration and preservation of Scripture (2 Tim 3:16, Ps 12:6). Jesus used the OT Scripture during His earthly ministry, and considered every word of it to be inspired. In Matt 5:18, He said, "Till heaven and earth pass, one jot or one tittle shall in no wise pass from the law, till all be fulfilled." This surely implies that the Hebrew Scriptures have been preserved through the centuries, to the extent that every bit of it has been left intact. If God has so providentially preserved the words of the OT Scriptures so that none of them is lost, will He not also preserve the NT Scriptures in the same way? Based on God's promises, we can say with good reason that we have the autographs of the NT in the wealth of extant manuscripts available today. Most of the extant NT manuscripts are of the Byzantine or Majority text-type which is well represented by the Textus Receptus. The rest of the manuscripts belong to the Alexandrian or Minority text-type, and are reflected in the Critical Text of Westcott/Hort, UBSGNT, and NANTG. We believe the Majority Text is the Preserved Text, and the Minority Text, the Corrupt Text.

The KJV Is Superior because of Its Godly and Able Translators

The King James Version is an excellent translation of the Holy Scriptures. It is a good fruit. It is a good fruit because it comes from a good tree (Matt 7:15–20). *The KJV is a good translation because of good translators*; in terms of their intellect and learning, they were brilliant; and in their faith and devotion towards God, they were vibrant.

GOOD FRUIT

One Version
KJV
Holy Bible

VITAL DOCTRINES PRESERVED

Deity of Christ

Virgin Birth of Christ

Redemption by the
Blood of the Lamb

GOOD TREE

Godly Translators

Good Technique

Textus Receptus

Good Text
Majority MSS

". . . every good tree bringeth forth good fruit."

There are two main books that talk about the KJV translators: (1) Alexander McClure, *Translator's Revived* (1858), and (2) Gustavus Paine, *The Men Behind the KJV* (1959).

There were a total of 54 scholars of the highest rank who translated the KJV. All of them were not only men of great learning but also of great piety. They were skilled in the biblical languages, and lived in a period when the English language was at its glorious height. It was a most providentially opportune time to translate the Scriptures into the English tongue.

The translators were divided into three groups: three OT and three NT. An OT-NT pair worked on their assigned books at Cambridge, another pair at Westminster, and another at Oxford. They began their work in 1604 and completed it in 1611—a total of seven years.

I do not think that today one can assemble such an august company of devout Bible scholars and theologians. I do believe that the translating of the KJV was a providential act of God just like the 16th century Reformation. Why do we have such confidence in the KJV? We have such confidence in the KJV because of the intellectual and spiritual qualities of the men that produced it.

The KJV Translators Were Men of Great Piety

The KJV translators evinced an intense love for God's Word. It is disheartening to know that there are people today who translate the Bible because of the love of money. Bible-publishing is a money-spinning enterprise.

Why do you think people spend time and energy to produce a new version once every few years? It can rake in millions of dollars. The KJV translators are thankfully not driven by money. They were driven by this desire that people need to read the Bible in its purity and accuracy in their own language. In their original preface to the KJV— "The Translators to the Reader"—they wrote, "But now what piety without truth? What truth (what saving truth) without the Word of God? What Word of God (whereof we may be sure) without Scripture? The Scriptures we are commanded to search (John 5:39; Isaiah 8:20). They are commended that searched and studied them (Acts 17:11 and 18:28). They are reproved that were unskilful in them, or slow to believe them

(Matthew 22:29, Luke 24:25). They can make us wise unto salvation (2 Timothy 3:15). If we be ignorant, they will instruct us; if out of the way, they will bring us home; if out of order, they will reform us; if in heaviness, comfort us; if dull, quicken us; if cold inflame us. ... Take up and read, take up and read the Scriptures ...".

Dr John Reynolds who is called "the father of the KJV" because it was he who proposed this project was a Puritan. And there were many others in the committee who were puritans. Now the puritans were famed for their piety. With such a reverent attitude and devotion to the Scriptures we are confident that they did not take their work lightly. Indeed, they did not frivolously throw out verses and passages, unlike the NIV which has removed so many verses from the Bible. Eg: Matt 18:11, "For the Son of man is come to save that which was lost." (In the NIV you have Matt 18:10, the next verse is not 11 but 12). Acts 8:37, "If thou believest with all thine heart, thou mayest. And he answered and said, I believe that Jesus Christ is the Son of God;" a total of 24 words missing! And such precious passages as John 7:58–8:11 on Jesus forgiving the woman taken in adultery and the last 12 verses of Mark are said to be not part of Scripture. What a lack of reverence for the Word of God by these NIV translators! We have scant confidence in these modern translators. There appears to be a general lack of reverence for the Scriptures in these modern translators. We rather trust the KJV.

The KJV Translators Were Men of Great Learning

Opponents of the KJV say that the KJ translators were outdated in their theology and in their learning. "We have better, more up-to-date theology," they say. What a deception and a false allegation! Spurgeon has well said, "There is nothing new in theology except that which is false." That is a true statement. Jeremiah's words continue to ring true: "Thus saith the LORD, Stand ye in the ways, and see, and ask for the old paths, where is the good way, and walk therein, and ye shall find rest for your souls" (Jer 6:16).

If you will read about the lives of the KJ translators you will be amazed by their intellectual and academic achievements. I dare say in terms of ability, they outstrip the modern translators any time. Let me just introduce you to a few of them:

Lancelot Andrews

Dr Andrews belonged to the Westminster team of translators, and was made chairman of the OT committee. Was Dr Andrews skilled in the OT languages? He was a graduate of Cambridge University where he devoted his time to the study of both modern and ancient languages, and to the study of theology. He was at home with 15 languages. (We are not talking about just a working knowledge of these languages. He was conversant with all 15). He was a very spiritual man, diligent in keeping his daily devotions (what we call QT). Do you know how he kept his QT? He would prayerfully read and meditate on the Scriptures, and then write his personal devotional thoughts in Greek. In other words, as he did his QT he wrote his RPG (*Read Pray Grow*), not in English but in Greek. Nowadays, there are pastors who do not even keep their QT, much less write devotional manuals, and if they do, how many would write them in the Greek language? Who can match Dr Andrews' spiritual sensitivity and linguistic superiority today?

William Bedwell

Dr Bedwell belonged to the Westminster team. He was an expert not only in Hebrew and Aramaic, but also in the cognate languages like Arabic, Persian, and other semitic languages. These extra-biblical languages are important in the translation of the OT because they are sister languages of Hebrew and Aramaic. Since they belong to the same family of semitic languages, knowing them will be helpful in identifying the meaning of certain rare words in the Bible. Dr Bedwell was so linguistically learned that he was able to produce an Arabic Lexicon or Dictionary (3 volumes), and a Persian Dictionary.

Henry Savile

Sir Henry Saville belonged to the Oxford team. He was involved in the translation of the NT. Saville became famous for his knowledge of the Greek language. He was Queen Elizabeth's personal Greek tutor. He was also equally proficient in Latin. He translated the histories of Cornelius Tacitus who was a Latin historian. Savile translated his work from Latin to English. He not only did this, but also edited the complete work of Chrysostom the famous Greek Church Father. His edition of Chrysostom amounted to eight immense folios. A folio is equivalent to the size of a volume of the Encyclopedia Brittannica; he had eight volumes of this size. A monumental work indeed! Do you find any of the modern translators producing such monumental works?

John Bois

Dr John Bois belonged to the Cambridge team. He was born into a very godly Christian family and was deeply influenced by his father. By the time he was five years old, Bois was able to read the Bible in Hebrew! By six years, he could write in Hebrew! Not only had he such talent for the Hebrew language, he also was equally skilled in the Greek so much so that when he was a freshman in St John's College, he wrote his personal letters to his Cambridge professors not in English but in Greek! Bois could compose his own essays in Greek when he was a student at Cambridge. It is thus no surprise that he later became professor of Greek at Cambridge. Can any of the modern translators say this of themselves? To be honest, they were giants; modern scholars are but dwarves. I would also venture to say that our modern translators are also pygmies compared to the KJV translators.

Moreover, we are living in an age when Bible Colleges and Seminaries are either giving up or diluting the study of the biblical languages. The Far Eastern Bible College requires all Master of Divinity (MDiv) students to go through the traditional language programme of three years of Greek and two years of Hebrew, but there are proudly accredited seminaries in the States today where you can obtain an MDiv without any of the languages, and no thesis to boot. Even such reputable seminaries as Dallas and Grace have removed significant chunks of their traditionally strong language departments to make room for more practice-oriented courses. Do the so-called Bible scholars of today really qualify to translate the Scriptures? How many of them if placed in 1600s would be selected to be part of the KJV translation committee?

The KJV is a result of God's providence. Consider Alexander McClure's "Evaluation of the KJ Translators and Translation." He wrote, "As to the capability of those men, we may say again, that by the good Providence of God, their work was undertaken in a fortunate time. Not only had the English language, that singular compound, then ripened to its full perfection, but the study of Greek, and of the oriental tongues, ... had then be carried to a greater extent in England than ever before or since. ... it is confidently expected that the reader of these pages will yield to the conviction, that all the colleges of Great Britain and America, even in this proud day of boastings, could not bring together the same number of divines equally qualified by learning and piety for the great undertaking. Few indeed are the living names worthy to be enrolled with those mighty men. It would be impossible to convene out of any one Christian denomination, or out of all, a body of translators, on whom the whole Christian community would bestow such confidence as is reposed upon that illustrious company, or who would prove themselves as deserving of such confidence" (*Translators Revived*, 63–4).

How do new versions and their translators compare to the KJV and its translators? According to McClure, "As to the Bible in its English form, it is safe to assume the impossibility of gathering a more competent body of translators, than those who did the work so well under King James's commission. ... And what has not been done by the most able and best qualified divines, is not likely to be done by obscure pedagogues, broken-down parsons, and sectaries of a single idea, and that a wrong one,—who, from different quarters, are talking big and loud of their 'amended,' 'improved,' and 'only correct' and reliable re-translations, and getting up 'American and Foreign Bible Unions' to print their sophomorical performances. How do such shallow adventurers appear along side of those venerable men ... The newly-risen versionists, with all their ambitious and pretentious vaunts are not worthy to 'carry satchels' after those masters of learning. Imagine our greenish contemporaries shut up with an Andrews, a Reynolds, a Ward, and a Bois, comparing notes on the meaning of the original Scriptures! It would soon be found, that all the aid of our moderns could render would be in snuffing the candles, ... Let tinkers stick to the baser metals; and heaven forefend that they should clout the vessels of the sanctuary with their clumsy patches" (*Translators Revived*, 233–4).

Consider Dean John William Burgon's confidence in the KJV. Dean Burgon, an Oxford scholar, was one of the greatest Bible defenders of the last century. In a time when Westcott and Hort sought to destroy the KJV by their corrupted Greek Text (today known as the eclectic text on which such versions as the RSV, NIV, and NASB are based). Dean Burgon was raised by the Lord to uphold and defend the KJV: "It may be confidently assumed that no 'revision' of our Authorized Version, however judiciously executed, will ever occupy the place in public esteem which is actually enjoyed by the work of the translators of 1611,— The noblest literary work in the Anglo-Saxon language" (*Revision Revised*, 113). He enjoined us "... to cling the closer to the priceless treasure which was bequeathed to them by the piety and wisdom of their fathers. ... How very seldom our Authorised Version is materially wrong; how faithful and trustworthy, on the contrary, it is throughout" (*Revision Revised*, 232).

Consider also Burgon's admiration of the KJ translators: "... the plain fact being that the men of 1611 produced a work of real genius: seizing with generous warmth the meaning and intention of the sacred Writers" (*Revision Revised*, 167). "Verily, those men understood their craft! 'There were giants in those days.' ... the Spirit of their God was mightily upon them" (*Revision Revised*, 196).

I want to echo the words of Dean Burgon on attempts to produce a new translation: "As something intended to supersede our present English Bible, we are thoroughly convinced that the project of a rival translation is not to be entertained for a moment. For ourselves, we deprecate it entirely" (*Revision Revised*, 113–4).

I dare say that the Bible scholars, theologians, and linguists of today fail to come even close to the calibre of scholarship and spirituality that we find in the KJ translators. I sincerely doubt that the KJV will ever be surpassed by a superior translation. In any case, until the Lord providentially raises up equally faithful and competent servants to give us a new version which is equally accurate and reliable, let us stick to the good old version—the KJV.

The KJV Is Superior because It Is an Accurate Translation

The KJV uses a superior method of translation. The KJV employs the verbal/formal over against the dynamic equivalence method of translation. The verbal/formal equivalence method is the only acceptable method for the translation of the Holy Scriptures. Why? Simply because the Bible is the verbally inspired Word of God. God gave a very serious warning in Rev 22:18, "For I testify unto every man that heareth the words of the prophecy of this book, If any man shall add unto these things, God shall add unto him the plagues that are written in this book:

And if any man shall take away from the words of the book of this prophecy, God shall take away his part out of the book of life, and out of the holy city, and from the things which are written in this book." In any attempt to translate the Scriptures, it is paramount that there should be no addition to, subtraction from, and changing of God's Word. It must be word-for-word, not thought-for-thought. The dynamic equivalence (a thought-for-thought) method may be well and good for other literature, but certainly not the Scriptures. The Bible's divine origin and its verbal inerrancy forbid it. "Blood" must be translated "blood," and not "death" (so TEV), and "Joseph" must be translated "Joseph," and not "the child's father" (so NIV).

The KJV Is Superior because It Is Faithful to Historic Protestant Theology

Those who say that all versions are good argue that there is no essential difference between the KJV and the modern versions in terms of theology. Although they admit that there are differences, they say that no vital doctrines are affected in all these new translations. I contend that this claim is false. We have already seen clear examples above of how these 20th century versions have unfaithfully manipulated the text affecting theology. We have discussed how certain doctrines have been affected. Let us recapitulate: (1) Inspiration of Scripture (2 Tim 3:16), (2) Preservation of Scripture (Ps 12:6), (3) Virgin Birth of Christ (Isa 7:14), (4) Eternal Generation of Christ (John 1:14,18, 3:16,18, 1 John 4:9), (5) the Holy Trinity (1 John 5:7–8), (6) the deity and humanity of Christ (1 Tim 3:16), and many others (see also D A Waite, *Defending the King James Bible*, 131–183).

Some will argue that the absence of the Johannine Comma (1 John 5:7f) does not affect the doctrine of the Trinity because there are many other biblical passages that teach it. The doctrine is thus not lost. While the doctrine may not be lost, a very strong testimony for it has surely been. Which other scriptural passage is as crystal clear as 1 John 5:7 in expressing the unity of the three Persons of the Godhead? We lose a very valuable proof-text by such flippant statements against the traditional preserved text in favour of the critical cut-up text. This is not a small matter as some would like to think. Paul warned, "a little leaven leaveneth the whole lump" (Gal 5:9). The 7% (NIV's Ken Barker says 2%) of missing words in the Scripture in the modern versions may be considered very little, but it is this little leaven that is destructive to God's Word, and to His Church.

The King James Bible vs the Hundred Versions

T. Tow   Lowell Mason

1. The Bi - ble is the Word of God,
2. God has pre - served it in the Text
3. Three hun - dred years it reigned su - preme,
4. An in - flux of hun - dred ver - sions
5. The Bi - ble is the Word of God,

In - er - rant and in - fal - li - ble,
Re - ceived by His Church ev - ery - where.
Un - til West - cott and Hort crept in,
By West - cott and Hort's text cor - rupt,
In - er - rant and in - fal - li - ble,

Pre - served for us from age to age.
Through good and faith - ful men of God,
And sowed the tares a - mongst the wheat,
Shall ne - ver stand up to the text,
Pre - served for us from age to age.

It stands God's Rock un - mov - a - ble.
The King James Bi - ble with - out peer.
And for a time they seemed to win.
That makes King James Bi - ble the best.
It stands God's Rock un - mov - a - ble.

THE SUPERIORITY OF THE KING JAMES VERSION   113

CHAPTER XI

FAQ ABOUT THE KJV

Q1. *Instead of using the KJV, can we use the New King James Version (NKJV)?*

The NKJV came into the scene in 1982. It claims to be an improvement of the old KJV. To its credit, the NKJV does not employ the dynamic but formal equivalence method of translation. It is thus a more reliable translation than the NIV. According to Arthur Farstad, the NKJV is more literal than the NIV, but more literary than the NASB.

Although better than the other modern versions available today, it is not superior to the old KJV because the NKJV fails to distinguish between the singular and plural of the 2nd personal pronoun (i.e. "you"). For instance, "thou art" is "you (sg) are," "ye are" is "you (pl) are," "thee" is "you (sg)," and "you (KJV)" is "you (pl)." The Greek differentiates between the singular and plural "you," and the old KJV renders them accordingly. "But the NKJV renders the singular "thee" to "you," and in so doing gives us a less precise translation. Eg: in Luke 22:31–32, the NKJV reads, "Simon, Simon! Indeed, Satan has asked for **you** (sg or pl?), that he may sift you as wheat. But I have prayed for **you** (sg or pl?), …" Cf KJV, "Simon, Simon, behold Satan hath desired to have **you** (pl), that he may sift you as wheat: But I have prayed for **thee** (sg), …".

In Isa 7:14 on the virgin birth, the NKJV reads, "Therefore the Lord Himself will give you (sg or pl? just Ahaz or faithful believers?) a sign, …". Since the NKJV does not distinguish between the singular and plural pronouns, it allows for a popular and very wrong interpretation of this verse which claims that the sign of the virgin birth was directly given to Ahaz the faithless king, and so must be fulfilled in his time. Walter Kaiser for example says that the virgin birth was fulfilled in Ahaz's wife, and the child born was Hezekiah! With the old KJV, it is clear that *the plural "you"* shifts the focus from Ahaz to the house of David hinting to us that Ahaz was not the recipient of this sign.

So, the NKJV though superior to most modern versions is still inferior to the old KJV. There is therefore no good reason to replace the KJV with the NKJV. For more information, read G W and D E Anderson, *The New King James Version* (London: Trinitarian Bible Society, 1995).

Q2. When you say the KJV is the only reliable and accurate Bible, are you implying that the Chinese, Tamil, Korean Bibles are not?

No, I am not implying that at all. We are also not saying that everyone in the whole wide world regardless of language must use only the English Bible. We are glad over the fact that the Bible is translated into so many languages. The Westminster Confession itself says that the Scriptures "are to be translated into the vulgar language of every nation." However, we must ensure that the translation used must be as faithful and accurate as possible.

Q3. Was King James a homosexual as alleged by anti-KJVists? If King James was such a man, does this not detract from the version that bears his name?

There are those who say that he was, and there are those who think otherwise. Before we pass judgment, we must hear from both sides viz, King James himself, and his accusers. We need concrete proof. Before we call someone a homosexual, we must be very sure he is so beyond doubt. But for argument's sake, let us say King James was gay. Being homosexual he would surely alter scriptural texts that speak against the sin of homosexuality. We do not find such alterations in the KJV. On the contrary, we find intact such passages as Rom 1:26–27 speaking out against *"vile affections; for even their women did change the natural use into that which is against nature: And likewise also the men, leaving the natural use of the woman, burned in their lust one toward another; men with men working that which is unseemly, and receiving in themselves that recompence of their error which was meet."* If King James were truly homosexual, he would be expected to change or dilute this passage. There was no such tampering. In any case, even if King James was gay, he was not among the translators, and had no part in the translating work. Whether he was a homosexual or not is a non-issue.

Lately, a scholarly 392-page book providing evidence in support of the godly character of King James is offered by Stephen A Coston Sr, *King*

James the VI of Scotland and the I of England: Unjustly Accused? (St Petersburg: KoenigsWort Incorporated, 1996).

Q4. The many archaic words of the KJV make it difficult for me to understand the Scriptures. Is this not good reason for me to change to a modern version?

No, it is not a good reason. The claim that the KJV has "many" archaic words and therefore not understandable is overstated. There are only about 200 archaic words in the KJV. These out-dated words comprise only 0.1% of the KJV. *The Defined KJB* published by The Bible For Today Press has the meanings of all the archaic words footnoted. For help, see also the "Bible Word List" published by the Trinitarian Bible Society, and *Archaic Words and the Authorized Version* by Laurence Vance.

Q5. The KJV is not as readable as the modern versions. Is this true?

After extensive research and study, D A Waite Jr says, "The entire KJV averages 1.31 syllables and 3.968 letters per word. This word length puts the KJV in the same readability category as the children's books ..." It is not true that the KJV is unreadable. For the details, go to D A Waite Jr, *The Comparative Readability of the Authorized Version* (Collingswood: Bible For Today, 1996). Those who want to improve their command of English would do well to use the KJV.

Q6. There are so many revisions on the KJV. So which KJV is the correct one?

The KJV was first published in 1611. However, there were revisions that followed soon after; all of which were completed in 1629. The revisions that occurred between 1611 and 1629 were due to printing errors. The KJV translators themselves, namely, Samuel Ward and John Bois, corrected these errors. In the course of typesetting, the printers have inadvertently left out words or phrases; all such manifest typographical errors were corrected. For example, Ps 69:32 of the 1611 edition read "good" instead of "God." This was clearly a printer's error, and was corrected in 1617.

Another revision of the KJV was done between 1762 and 1769. This revision had to do with spelling. For example, old forms that had an "e" after verbs, and "u" instead of "v," and "f" for "s" were all standardised to conform to modern spelling. For example, "feare" is "fear," "mooued" is "moved," and "euill" is "evil," and "alfo," is "also." All these Gothic and

German spelling peculiarities have been Romanised by 1769. It is important to note that the 1769 edition is essentially the same as the 1611. There are not two or more KJVs but only one, and the one that is used today is the 1769 edition. (See Waite, *Defending the King James Bible*, 237–8.)

Q7. Aren't KJV-only or KJV-superiority advocates ignorant or unscholarly people?

The accusation of not being up-to-date or unscholarly is leveled against KJV advocates by neo-evangelicals especially. If you do not buy their brand of mixed-up modernistic cum evangelical scholarship, and disagree with their liberal presuppositions, you are labeled an "ignoramus." Although there are KJV extremists who have zeal but not knowledge, there are many who do their research, are proficient in the biblical languages, and are well-trained in theology. More importantly, all are ardent Christians who love the Lord, and His Word.

This stigma of being called an "ignoramus" if you support the KJV and oppose WH was faced by **Alfred Martin** (former Vice-President of Moody Bible Institute) when he was at Dallas Theological Seminary. So he decided to write his ThD dissertation to prove the WH textual critical theory wrong. The title of his dissertation written in 1951 was, "A Critical Examination of the Westcott-Hort Textual Theory." This is what he wrote, "The present generation of Bible students, having been reared on Westcott and Hort, have for the most part accepted the theory without independent or critical examination. To the average student of the Greek New Testament today it is unthinkable to question the theory at least in its basic premises. Even to imply that one believes the Textus Receptus to be nearer the original text than the Westcott-Hort text is, lays one open to the suspicion of gross ignorance or unmitigated bigotry. ...

"At precisely the time when liberalism was carrying the field in the English churches the theory of Westcott and Hort received wide acclaim. These are not isolated facts. Recent contributions on the subject—that is, in the present century—following mainly the Westcott-Hort principles and method, have been made largely by men who deny the inspiration of the Bible. ...

"Textual criticism cannot be divorced entirely from theology. No matter how great a Greek scholar a man may be, or no matter how great an authority on the textual evidence, his conclusions must always be opened to suspicion if he does not accept the Bible as the very Word of God. ...

"The great difficulty in New Testament textual criticism today, which makes it impossible for Bible-believing Christians to be sanguine about the results of present research, is the almost universally held view among critics of the relative nature of truth. Textual criticism has become more and more subjective since Westcott and Hort opened the door of subjectivism wide" (David Cloud, *Myths About the King James Bible* [Oak Harbor: Way of Life, 1993], 18–9).

We thank the Lord that some anti-TR/KJV scholars later changed their position. They were honest about their initial blindness or ignorance, and spoke for the TR/KJV after knowing the truth. One such man is **William Bruner**, ThM, PhD. In a letter to D O Fuller he said, "... you wrote me a very kind letter and sent me some sample materials from your book *Which Bible?*. You might as well have been shooting a pop gun at a stone wall. My mind was so strongly fortified in the doctrine of Westcott and Hort that I could not for one moment consider the King James Bible. Had I not studied Textual Criticism under the great Dr. A.T. Robertson? I thought that you were just one of those die-hard Fundamentalists who were striving to keep the Christian world under the bondage of traditionalism. Such men are interested only in pleasing the people by catering to their ignorance, prejudice and sentimentality! But just a few weeks ago I happened to read your two books, *Which Bible?* and *True or False?*. For the first time a little new light shone in. I saw that there is another side of the argument. Dr Robertson had not given us all the facts" (Ibid, 4).

Apparently there has been *a conspiracy of silence!* This silence is promoted in most Bible colleges and seminaries when NT Introduction and NT Exegesis are taught. This is testified by **D A Waite**, ThD, PhD, who wrote, "For about twenty years I was in darkness about this issue. I knew nothing of it from roughly 1951 to 1971. ... I was at Dallas Theological Seminary from 1948–1952. That was my Master of Theology. Then I stayed an extra year, 1953. Throughout those years we were simply told to use the Westcott and Hort Greek New Testament, which we did in the Greek classes. It was the actual text Westcott and Hort developed. It was not simply another text—the Nestles [sic] Text or the Souter Text—but it was Westcott and Hort. And *I didn't know there was any other Greek text.* ...

"I majored in classic [sic] Greek and Latin at the University of Michigan, 1945–48. Took three years to get my four years of work. I went summer and winter, so that I could marry my wife. Then I came to Dallas Seminary. I was learning New Testament Greek, and I didn't pay much heed to the text. I didn't care. I just wanted to learn the forms and get good grades, which I did. But I did not examine the textual base that we were using. *I just assumed that was the only one to use.*

"You ask the question, then, how I came to understand the Bible version issue... , my mother-in-law to be, Mrs. Gertrude Grey Sanborn, gave me the book *God Wrote Only One Bible*. I didn't say or think too much about it. I didn't study it at that time, but that was my first introduction. Then as I was teaching as professor of Greek at Shelton College in Cape Maine [sic], New Jersey, one of my pupils, Sandra Devos—Sandra Phillips, I think, was her name then—said that there was a book in our library at Shelton by Dean John William Burgon that defends not only the King James Bible, but also the Greek text, the Received Text, that underlies the Bible.

" 'Have you ever seen that book, Dr Waite?' she asked me. I said, 'Well, no, I haven't.' I think I might have looked at it; I might have glanced at it. I thought to myself, 'Here is an interesting thing. Here is the first book that I have seen that says there is a difference in the Greek text that the modern versions are using, and that the King James Bible that underlies it, the Textus Receptus, is superior to the Westcott and Hort type text, or to the critical text.'

"... Then about that time, I think it was about 1969 or 1970, along in there, Dr. Fuller came out with his book *Which Bible?*. I read that. Also I looked at at least one of the books by Dr. Edward F. Hills—*Believing Bible Study*. I don't think I saw at the time his other book, *The Defense of the King James Bible* [sic].

"So in 1971, having read these various books, I was deeply convicted and convinced that the King James Bible and the Greek text that underlies it, as well as the Hebrew text—although I got into the

Hebrew text a little bit later—but I was convinced that the Greek text that underlies the New Testament of the King James Bible was the accurate text to use. ...

"So can you say the first twenty years, from 1951–71, I was in somewhat of a daze, somewhat of a darkness, concerning the issues. Then from 1971–91, twenty more years, I have been writing, I have been studying, I have been preaching, I have been teaching, I have been debating, I have been arguing, I have been talking about, I have been preaching from, I have continued to memorize from and believe the King James Bible and the text that underlies that Bible. So for twenty years I've been a stalwart defender of that Book" (Ibid, 4–5; see also D A Waite, *Defending the King James Bible*, 218–9).

Consider also the testimony of **Edward F Hills** (BD, Westminster, ThM, Columbia, ThD, Harvard). On how he became a KJV believer, Dr Hills wrote, "I have been interested in the problem of New Testament textual criticism since my high school days in the 1920's. At that time I began to read the commentaries of Charles Hodge, books that were a part of my Presbyterian heritage. I noticed that Hodge would sometimes mention variant readings, most however, just to show that he was knowledgeable, for he rarely departed from 'the common text' (textus receptus) and 'our English version' (King James). Even so my curiosity was roused, so that in 1931, when I was a sophomore at Yale University I took down C. R. Gregory's *Canon and Text of the NT* from a library shelf and began to read. I was dismayed at the large number of verses that, according to Gregory and his teachers Westcott and Hort, must be rejected from the Word of God. Nor was I much comforted by Gregory's assurance that the necessary damage had been done and the rest of the text had been placed on an unassailable basis. How could I be sure of this? It seemed to me that the only way to gain assurance on this point was to go to Westminster Seminary and study the question under the tutelage of Dr. Machen, who preached in New Haven rather frequently in those days, talking to Yale students at least twice.

"When I began to study New Testament textual criticism at Westminster (under Dr. Stonehouse) I found that the first day or so was mainly devoted to praising Dr. B. B. Warfield. He was lauded for being among the first to recognize the 'epoch making' importance of the theory of Westcott and Hort and for establishing the Westcott and Hort tradition at Princeton Seminary, a tradition which was now being faithfully perpetuated at Westminster Seminary. To me, however, all this was very puzzling. Dr. Warfield was a renowned defender of the Reformed faith and of the Westminster Confession, yet in the department of New Testament textual criticism he agreed entirely with liberals such as Westcott, Hort and C. R. Gregory. He professed to agree with the statement of the Westminster Confession that the Scriptures by God's 'singular care and providence' had been 'kept pure in all ages', but it was obvious that this providential preservation of the Scripture was of no importance to Dr. Warfield when he actually began to deal with the problems of the New Testament. When he engaged in New Testament textual criticism, Dr. Warfield ignored the providential preservation of the Scriptures and treated the text of the New Testament as he would the text of any book or writing. 'It matters not whether the writing before us be a letter from a friend, or an inscription from Carchemish, or a copy of a morning newspaper, or Shakespeare, or Homer, or the Bible.'

"I may be reading back into my student days some of my later thinking, but it seems to me that even at that time I could see that the logic of Warfield's naturalistic New Testament textual criticism led steadily downward toward modernism and unbelief. For if the providential preservation of the Scriptures was not important for the study of the New Testament text, then it could not have been important for the history of the New Testament text. And if it had not been important for the history of the New Testament, then it must have been non-existent. It could not have been a fact. And if the providential preservation of the Scriptures was not a fact, why should the infallible inspiration of the Scriptures be regarded as a fact? Why would God infallibly inspire a book and then decline to preserve it providentially? For example, why would God infallibly inspire the Gospel of Mark and then permit (as Warfield thought possible) the ending of it (describing the resurrection appearances of Christ) to be lost?

"Why was Dr. Warfield so inconsistent in the realm of New Testament textual criticism? Dr. Van Til's course in apologetics enabled me to supply the answer to this question. Dr. Warfield's inconsistency was part of his scholastic inheritance, an error which had been handed down to him from the middle-ages. Let me explain. During the middle-ages the school men tried to reconcile the philosophy of Aristotle with the dogmas of the Roman Catholic Church by separating faith from reason and praying from thinking. While dealing with dogma, faith and prayer were appropriate, but the study of philosophy was reason's province. So the medieval schoolmen contended, and soon this doctrine of the separation of faith from reason became generally accepted throughout the medieval Roman Catholic Church.

"The Protestant Reformers were fully occupied with other matters. Hence they spent but little time combating this medieval, Roman Catholic error of the separation of faith and reason. Hence this false scholastic doctrine survived the Reformation and soon became embedded in the thinking of conservative Protestants everywhere. In the 18th century Butler and Paley built their apologetic systems on this false principle of the separation of faith and reason, and in the 19th century, at Princeton and other conservative theological seminaries, this scholastic principle even governed the curriculum and the way in which the several subjects were taught. Systematic theology, practical theology and homiletics were placed in one box labeled FAITH. All the other subjects, including New Testament textual criticism, biblical introduction, apologetics and philosophy, were placed in another box labeled REASON.

"We see now why Dr. Warfield was so inconsistent. We see why he felt himself at liberty to adopt the naturalistic theories of Westcott and Hort and did not perceive that in so doing he was contradicting the Westminster Confession and even his own teaching in the realm of systematic theology. The reason was that Dr. Warfield kept these subjects in separate boxes. Like an authentic, medieval scholastic, he kept his systematic theology and the Westminster Confession in his FAITH box and his New Testament textual criticism in his REASON box. Since he never tried to mingle the contents of these two boxes, he was never fully aware of the discrepancies in his thinking.

"When I began to study New Testament textual criticism at Westminster in 1935, I noticed another thing. Almost as much time was spent in disparaging Dean Burgon as in praising Dr. Warfield. This again aroused my curiosity. Who was this Dean Burgon? Upon investigation, I found that he had been a British scholar that had not fitted into the usual scholastic mold. He had not kept his theology and his New Testament textual criticism in two separate boxes, but had actually dared to make his theology the guiding principle of his New Testament textual criticism. For this he was pronounced 'unscholarly'.

"Actually, however, he was merely following the logic of faith. He believed that the New Testament was the infallibly inspired Word of God. Hence it had been preserved down through the ages by God's special providence, not secretly in holes and caves and on forgotten library shelves but publicly in the usage of God's Church. Hence the text found in the vast majority of the New Testament manuscripts is the true text because this is the text that has been used by God's Church. As soon as I began to read Burgon's works, I was impressed by this logic of faith and also by the learned arguments by which Burgon refuted the contention of Tischendorf, Tregelles, Westcott, Hort, etc. Finally, after some years of hesitation, I definitely committed myself to his view in 1952. ...

"Therefore, the true New Testament text is found today in the majority of the Greek New Testament manuscripts, in the Textus Receptus, and in the King James Version and other faithful translations of the Textus Receptus. And therefore also this same preserving providence operating today through the agency of all those true believers, however humble, who retain and defend the King James Version."

Another such story is that of Dr **S Franklin Logsdon** (1907–87) who translated the NASB. Dr Logsdon in his testimony—"From NASV to KJV"—wrote, "Back in 1956–57 Mr. F. Dewey Lockman of the Lockman Foundation [contacted me. He was] one of the dearest friends we've ever had for 25 years, a big man, some 300 pounds, snow white hair, one of the most terrific businessmen I have ever met. I always said he was like Nehemiah; he was building a wall. You couldn't get in his way when he had his mind on something; he went right to it; he couldn't be daunted. I never saw anything like it; most unusual man. I spent weeks and weeks and weeks in their home, real close friends of the family.

"Well, he discovered that the copyright [on the American Standard Version of 1901] was just as loose as a fumbled ball on a football field. Nobody wanted it. The publishers didn't want it. It didn't get anywhere.

Mr. Lockman got in touch with me and said, 'Would you and Ann come out and spend some weeks with us, and we'll work on a feasibility report; I can pick up the copyright to the 1901 if it seems advisable.'

"Well, up to that time I thought the Westcott and Hort was the text. You were intelligent if you believed the Westcott and Hort. Some of the finest people in the world believe in that Greek text, the finest leaders that we have today. You'd be surprised; if I told you you wouldn't believe it. They haven't gone into it just as I hadn't gone into it; [they're] just taking it for granted.

"At any rate we went out and started on a feasibility report, and I encouraged him to go ahead with it. I'm afraid I'm in trouble with the Lord, because I encouraged him to go ahead with it. We laid the groundwork; I wrote the format; I helped to interview some of the translators; I sat with the translators; I wrote the preface. When you see the preface to the New American Standard, those are my words.

"I got one of the fifty deluxe copies which were printed; mine was number seven, with a light blue cover. But it was rather big and I couldn't carry it with me, and I never really looked at it. I just took for granted that it was done as we started it, you know, until some of my friends across the country began to learn that I had some part in it and they started saying, 'What about this; what about that?'

"Dr. David Otis Fuller in Grand Rapids [Michigan]. I've known him for 35 years, and he would say (he would call me Frank; I'd call him Duke), 'Frank, what about this? You had a part in it; what about this; what about that?' And at first I thought, Now, wait a minute; let's don't go overboard; let's don't be too critical. You know how you justify yourself the last minute.

"But I finally got to the place where I said, 'Ann, I'm in trouble; I can't refute these arguments; it's wrong; it's terribly wrong; it's frightfully wrong; and what am I going to do about it?' Well, I went through some real soul searching for about four months, and I sat down and wrote one of the most difficult letters of my life, I think.

"I wrote to my friend Dewey, and I said, 'Dewey, I don't want to add to your problems,' (he had lost his wife some three years before; I was there for the funeral; also a doctor had made a mistake in operating on a cataract and he had lost the sight of one eye and had to have an operation on the other one; he had a slight heart attack; had sugar diabetes; a man seventy-four years of age) 'but I can no longer ignore these criticisms I am hearing and I can't refute them. The only thing I can do—and dear Brother, I haven't a thing against you and I can witness at the judgment of Christ and before men wherever I go that you were 100% sincere,' (he wasn't schooled in language or anything; he was just a businessman; he did it for money; he did it conscientiously; he wanted it absolutely right and he thought it was right; I guess nobody pointed out some of these things to him) 'I must under God renounce every attachment to the New American Standard.' "

For other scholars who hold to the KJV-only position, see *Myths About the King James Bible: Myth #5, True Scholars Reject the Received Text* by David Cloud.

Q8. What do you think of Gail Riplinger, and her recent book—New Age Bible Versions?

Riplinger is to be commended for defending the KJV. Her book, however, has received mixed reviews. The Trinitarian Bible Society, in a review of her book, wrote, "Mrs. Riplinger's book contains no bibliography and many of the endnotes lack such necessary documentation as author and publisher. In addition, the book contains many factual errors, false innuendos, mistakes in logic, misquotations and instances of misleading research as well as general English language errors. ... This does not mean that there is no value to the verifiable, truthful or factual statements made in this book; however, many things in this book are without support and therefore untrustworthy." (The full report can be obtained from the Trinitarian Bible Society, 1710 Richmond NW, Grand Rapids MI 49504, USA.)

This is what Dave Hunt—author of *The Seduction of Christianity*—wrote about Riplinger's *New Age Bible Versions*, "Those who have a preference for the KJV, as we do, will find no encouragement in Riplinger's endeavor. Her writing is driven by a misleading style and loaded with contrived 'evidence.' She starts off misrepresenting people and continues to do so throughout the entire book" (*Berean Call*, May '94).

David W Cloud—editor of *O Timothy* magazine—also criticised Riplinger's book, "For every person who turns from modern versions due to the influence of this book, I praise the Lord. Let me say very plainly at the outset ... I do not believe *New Age Bible Versions* is a dangerous book; I believe it is an undependable book" (*O Timothy* 11:8 [1994]).

D A Waite is of a different opinion. He says, "Mrs Gail Riplinger has documented all 700 pages of her book, *New Age Bible Versions*. ... I believe there is tremendous value in her book. It is a book that has sold over 100,000 copies. It has been used to awaken many people as to the Bible version perversion" (*Foes of the King James Bible Refuted* [Collingswood: Bible For Today, 1997], 49). Waite no longer recommends Riplinger.

Q9. What is Bob Jones University's position on the Bible versions?

Bob Jones University (BJU) is a fundamentalist and separatist school. However, in the area of Bible versions, it is not fundamental but neo-evangelical. The school has rejected the unequivocal KJV-only stance to take a neo-evangelical, middle-of-the-road view that modern versions based on the corrupt Westcott-Hort (WH) text are good too. This is reflected in the BJU position statement on the Bible, and the recently published *From the Mind of God to the Mind of Man* book (henceforth *The Mind*) edited by BJU man—J B Williams (for a full critique, see Appendix). Briefly, BJU takes the following neutral as well as contradictory positions:

(1) *Inspiration Yes, Preservation No*: BJU believes that inspiration extends only to the autographs (i.e., the actual manuscripts penned by the biblical writers), and not the apographs (i.e., copies). God inspired His Word but did not preserve it. According to BJU, one can only be sure that every doctrine in the Bible is preserved, but not every word.

(2) *KJV Yes, TR No*: BJU says that the KJV is its classroom text. Teachers and students use the KJV in the classroom. That is good. What is not good however is that although BJU supports the KJV, its teachers generally undermine the Preserved Hebrew and Greek Text (i.e., TR) on which it is based. BJU allows for the Westcott and Hort view that such precious passages as the last 12 verses of Mark, the woman taken in adultery (John 7:53–8:11), and John's Trinitarian statement (1 John 5:7) are not part of inspired Scripture.

(3) *KJV Yes, Modern Versions Yes Too*: BJU adopts the KJV as its classroom text, but it also approves of such versions as the American Standard Version (ASV) and New American Standard Bible (NASB). Note that the ASV is the American twin of the English Revised Version (RV) translated by WH in 1881. The NASB, born out of the ASV, is a new but nonetheless bad fruit of the corrupt WH tree.

Given its equivocal position, it would not be surprising if down the road the school abandons the KJV altogether.

Q10. *Which Colleges or Seminaries hold to the KJV-superiority position?*

Besides Far Eastern Bible College, there is Pensacola Christian College and Theological Seminary, 250 Brent Lane, Box 18000, Pensacola FL 32523, USA. "At Pensacola Christian College, we believe in the plenary, verbal inspiration of the Bible, and it is our practice to use only the King James Version in the pulpit and in classroom instruction. We believe the Textus Receptus is a superior text, and we use it for Greek instruction." Pensacola has come up very strongly against fundamental colleges and seminaries that either merely pay lip service to the KJV, or undermine it altogether by rejecting the traditional text in favour of the modern but corrupt eclectic text. Get a hold of these three excellent video lectures on the KJV issue by Dr Dell Johnson, Dr Theodore Letis, and Dr Michael Bates: (1) "The Leaven in Fundamentalism," (2) "The Bible ... The Text is the Issue," and (3) "The Bible Preserved ... from Satan's Attacks."

Puritan Reformed Theological Seminary under its President, Dr Joel Beeke, takes the Confessional position on the text underlying the KJV. Dr Beeke says, "A principal reason for retaining the KJV is the text from which it is translated. The extant evidence justifies the conclusion that the Greek edition used by the KJV translators represents the best tradition preserved in the majority of the witnesses to the text of the New Testament." The Puritan Reformed Theological Seminary is located at 2965 Leonard Street NE, Grand Rapids, MI 49525, USA.

CHAPTER XII

CONCLUSION

International Council of Christian Churches' Resolution on the KJV

The Bible-Presbyterian Church of Singapore and the Far Eastern Bible College is part of the 20th Century Reformation Movement of the International Council of Christian Churches (ICCC) started by the great American fundamentalist—Dr Carl McIntire. In the ICCC 16th World Congress, the following statement on the Holy Scriptures and the Bible Translations was issued:

"Believing the Holy Scriptures on the originals to be fully inspired with its words and genders and being complete as God's revelation to man without error;

"Believing that God not only inspired the Bible without errors in fact, doctrine and judgment but preserved the Scriptures in all ages for all eternity as the Westminster Confession of Faith standard says—'the O.T. in Hebrew and the N.T. in Greek' ... 'being immediately inspired by God and by his singular care and providence kept pure in all ages are therefore authentical ....'" They are to be translated into the vulgar language of every nation unto which they come;'

"Believing the Holy Spirit, the third person of the Trinity, gave us a supernatural gift, and both inspired and preserved it. By inspired we mean that the Holy Spirit moved in the hearts of its human authors that they recorded the very words that God wanted written in the Bible using the personality and background of its writers but without error. 'For the prophecy came not in old time by the will of man; but holy men of God spake as they were moved by the Holy Ghost.' II Pet 1:21;

"Believing God safeguarded the Bible in times past and will continue to do so in the future and all eternity. He preserved on

Scripture, the Bible. 'Heaven and earth shall pass away but my words shall not pass away;' Matt 24:35;

"Believing the O.T. has been preserved in the Masoretic text and the N.T. in the Textus Receptus, combined they gave us the complete Word of God. The King James Version in English has been faithfully translated from these God-preserved manuscripts. Other good Protestant versions have been translated around the world in many languages based on the Masoretic and Textus Receptus until 1881 when Drs. Westcott and Hort used a shorter text removing many words, phrases and sections by following the eclectic watered down polluted Vaticanus and Sinaiticus manuscripts;

"These manuscripts differ widely among themselves and with others amount to less than 5% of the manuscript evidence. God preserved the Textus Receptus in the majority text with 95%. This is called the traditional, or majority text. It is also called Eastern Byzantine text and also the manuscripts that have the longer and fuller texts;

"Believing that these longer texts are corroborated by the early century versions from the Greek that were closer in the time of the original Greek manuscripts that have been lost usage in the providence of God. Some of these are the Armenian, Old Latin, the Syriac Peshitta and the Latin Vulgate; these date much before or close to the Vaticanus short version and Sinaiticus;

"Believing the letters that the early church fathers wrote to the churches and to their colleagues corroborate that the 1000's of quotes from the Scriptures they used, are from the traditional longer texts of the Textus Receptus;

"Believing the manuscript evidence is on the side of the Textus Receptus and with the many new books that explained this better than in times past and give more documentary manuscript evidence;

"We the International Council of Christian Churches meeting in Jerusalem, 8–14 November 2000 strongly urge the churches in their pulpits and people at large, to continue to use the time honoured and faithful longer translations and not the new shorter versions that follow in too many places the short eclectic texts. These are very similar to the shorter Westcott and Hort texts that remove or cast doubt on so many passages and words. Furthermore we are not against new versions as such but believe all true and faithful versions must be based on the traditional longer texts that the Holy Spirit preserved through the early century versions, the early church fathers and the faithful Textus Receptus."

We also fully concur with the Bible Resolution passed at the ICCC 50th Anniversary Congress held in Amsterdam, The Netherlands, August 11–14, 1998 which reads,

"WHEREAS despite the fact that there are over 150 so-called "versions" of the Bible extant around the world today, there have been no new discoveries of ancient texts to legitimize this plethora of modern "versions" pouring off the presses and being sold as the "latest" Bible, and

"WHEREAS a single exception to this has been the discovery of the now-famous Dead Sea Scrolls in the 1940's in caves on the Judean mountain range and contained in clay jars with the texts written on leather and papyrus, and

"WHEREAS fragments of all the books of the Hebrew Bible (except Esther) confirm almost to the letter the accuracy of the Authorized King James Version of the Old Testament, and

"WHEREAS most of the modern versions are based upon the discredited and perverted Westcott and Hort transcription and not on the Textus Receptus (The Received Text) attested to by scholars for over 300 years, from which the Authorized King James Version was translated by the greatest theologians and textual critics of 17th Century England, who were academic experts, indeed, in Hebrew, Greek and Aramaic, and

"WHEREAS self-styled theologians who reject the inerrancy and inspiration of the Scriptures have gone so far as to make a looseleaf notebook and tear out those passages they do not accept, even organizing what they designate as 'Jesus Seminars' across the United States in which they declare that Jesus never did and said the things recorded in the four Gospels; and that the Gospel of John is the worst and is 90 percent fiction, and the obedient secular press quotes them from coast-to-coast, and

"WHEREAS this same KING JAMES VERSION has been used around the world by an overwhelming majority of Christian Clergymen, Evangelists, Bible Teachers, Missionaries and Youth Leaders to bring millions of people to have a saving knowledge of the Lord Jesus Christ for more than three centuries,

"BE IT THEREFORE RESOLVED, that the International Council of Christian Churches, assembled in the historic English Reformed Church in Amsterdam, The Netherlands, observing its 50th Anniversary, August 11–15, 1998, urge all Bible-believing churches worldwide to use only the Authorized KING JAMES VERSION in their services and in their teaching ministry, and warn the followers of Christ against these innumerable 'new' bibles which are not translations at all, but revisions conforming to the personal bias and views of those who have originated them and who are profiting by commercial sales of such."

Is there any who calls himself a fundamentalist that will scoff at this resolution? There are indeed "fundamentalists" who simply pay lip-service to the doctrine of biblical inspiration and preservation. In the same breath they say yes and no to the Word of God they claim to uphold: "Yes to the KJV; No to the Textus Receptus" (note: the Textus Receptus is the Greek Text underlying the KJV). Dr Carl McIntire, President of the ICCC did well to quote J Gresham Machen in the January 17, 1957 issue of the *Christian Beacon*, "The worst sin today is to say that you agree with the Christian faith and believe in the Bible, but then make common cause with those who deny the basic facts of Christianity. Never was it more obviously true that he that is not with Christ is against Him." How can they who claim to believe in a verbally inspired Bible support Westcott and Hort—the Bible and Christ denying progenitors of our modern English versions? Westcott and Hort were modernists and Mariolators, supporters of Freud and Darwin. They applied the scissors to the traditional and preserved Greek NT used and accepted by God's people down through the ages. This unregenerate duo hoodwinked the Church into accepting their mutilated text, save Dean John William Burgon who in godly jealousy rose to debunk Westcott and Hort in his masterly treatise—*The Revision Revised*.

Therefore, fundamentalists who continue to promote the Westcott-Hort Greek text which is now renamed "Eclectic," and all the corrupt English "Bibles" that flood the Christian market are not fighting against Satan, but against Christ. I repeat the words of Machen, "The worst sin today is to say that you agree with the Christian Faith and believe in the Bible (viz, the KJV), but make common cause with those who deny the basic facts of Christianity (viz, Westcott and Hort). Never was it more obviously true that he that is not with Christ is against Him." "When the enemy shall come in like a flood, the spirit of the LORD shall lift up a standard against him" (Isa 59:19). "For we can do nothing against the truth, but for the truth" (2 Cor 13:8). "Nevertheless the foundation of God standeth sure, having this seal, The Lord knoweth them that are his. And, Let every one that nameth the name of Christ depart from iniquity" (2 Tim 2:19).

Acknowledgement and Recommendation of Sources

Anderson, G W. *The Greek New Testament.* London: Trinitarian Bible Society, 1994.

_____, and D E Anderson. *The Authorised Version.* London: Trinitarian Bible Society, nd.

_____. *New International Version: What Today's Christian Needs to Know About the NIV.* London: Trinitarian Bible Society, nd.

_____. *The New King James Version.* London: Trinitarian Bible Society, 1995.

_____. *A Textual Key to the New Testament: A List of Omissions and Changes.* London: Trinitarian Bible Society, 1993.

_____. *Why 1 John 5:7–8 is in the Bible.* London: Trinitarian Bible Society, 1993.

Bruce, F F. *History of the Bible in English.* 3rd edition. New York: Oxford University, 1978.

Burgon, John William. *The Revision Revised: A Refutation of Westcott and Hort's False Greek Text and Theory.* Collingswood NJ: Dean Burgon Society, nd.

_____, and J P Green Sr. *Unholy Hands on the Bible: An Introduction to Textual Criticism Including the Complete Works of John W Burgon, Dean of Chichester.* Volume 1. Lafayette IN: Sovereign Grace Trust Fund, 1990.

Cloud, David W. *Examining "The King James Only Controversy."* Oak Harbor WA: Way of Life Literature, 1998.

_____. *For Love of the Bible: The Battle for the King James Version and the Received Text from 1800 to Present.* Oak Harbor WA: Way of Life Literature, 1995.

_____. *Modern Bible Versions: A Concise but Thorough Overview of the Issue of Bible Texts and Versions.* Oak Harbor WA: Way of Life Literature, 1994.

_____. *Modern Versions Founded Upon Apostasy.* Oak Harbor WA: Way of Life Literature, 1995.

_____. *Myths About the Modern Bible Versions.* Oak Harbor WA: Way of Life Literature, 1999.

_____. Editor. *Way of Life Encyclopedia on the Bible and Christianity Based upon the King James Bible and Written from an Uncompromising, Bible-believing Position.* Oak Harbor WA: Way of Life Literature, 1993.

_____. *What About Ruckman?* 2nd edition. Oak Harbor: Way of Life Literature, 1995.

Coston Sr, Stephen A. *King James: Unjustly Accused?* St Petersburg FL: KoenigsWort Incorporated, 1996.

Ecumenism and the United Bible Societies. London: Trinitarian Bible Society, nd.

Farrell, Hugh. *Rome and the RSV.* London: Trinitarian Bible Society, 1968.

Fuller, David Otis. Editor. *True or False?* Grand Rapids MI: Grand Rapids International Publications, 1973.

_____. Editor. *Which Bible?* Grand Rapids MI: Grand Rapids International Publications, 1975.

God Manifest in the Flesh (1 Timothy 3:16): Examination of a Disputed Passage. London: Trinitarian Bible Society, nd.

Green Sr, Jay P. *Unholy Hands on the Bible: An Examination of Six Major New Versions.* Volume 2. Lafayette IN: Sovereign Grace Trust Fund, 1992.

Hills, Edward F. *Believing Bible Study.* 2nd edition. Des Moines IA: Christian Research Press, 1977.

_____. *The King James Version Defended.* Des Moines IA: Christian Research Press, 1984.

Johnson, Dell, J Michael Bates, and Theodore Letis. *The Bible—The Text is the Issue.* Videotape. Pensacola FL: Pensacola Christian College, 1997.

_____. *The Bible Preserved from Satan's Attack.* Videotape. Pensacola FL: Pensacola Christian College, 1996.

_____ and Theodore Letis. *The Leaven in Fundamentalism: A History of the Bible Text Issue in Fundamentalism.* Videotape. Pensacola FL: Pensacola Christian College, 1998.

Letis. Theodore P. *The Ecclesiastical Text: Text Criticism, Biblical Authority and the Popular Mind.* Philadelphia: The Institute for Renaissance and Reformation Biblical Studies, 1997.

_____. Editor. *The Majority Text: Essays and Reviews in the Continuing Debate.* Philadelphia: The Institute for Renaissance and Reformation Biblical Studies, 1987.

_____. *A New Hearing for the Authorized Version.* 2nd edition. Philadelphia: The Institute for Renaissance and Reformation Biblical Studies, 1998.

Madden, D K. *A Critical Examination of the New American Standard Bible.* Tasmania Australia: np, 1981.

Maynard, Michael. *A History of the Debate Over 1 John 5:7–8: A Tracing of the Longevity of the Comma Johanneum, With Evaluations of Arguments Against its Authenticity.* Tempe AZ: Comma Publications, 1995.

McClure, Alexander. *Translators Revived.* Mobile AL: R E Publications, nd.

Miller, Edward. *A Guide to the Textual Criticism of the New Testament.* Collingswood NJ: Dean Burgon Society, 1979.

Morris, Henry M. *A Creationist's Defense of the King James Bible.* El Cajon CA: Institute for Creation Research, 1996.

_____. *The Defender's Study Bible: KJV* (Grand Rapids MI: World Publishing, 1995).

Moorman, Jack. *Modern Bibles—The Dark Secret.* Los Osos CA: Fundamental Evangelistic Association, nd.

Paine, Gustavus S. *The Men Behind the KJV.* Grand Rapids MI: Baker Book House, 1977.

Paisley, Ian R K. *My Plea for the Old Sword: The Unsurpassable Preeminency of the English Authorised Version (KJV) of the Holy Bible.* Greenville SC: Emerald House, 1997.

Radmacher, Earl, and Zane C Hodges. *The NIV Reconsidered: A Fresh Look at a Popular Translation.* Dallas TX: Redencion Viva, 1990.

Ray, James Jasper. *God Wrote Only One Bible.* Junction City OR: The Eye Opener, 1980.

Sorenson, David H. *Touch Not the Unclean Thing: The Bible Translation Controversy and the Principle of Separation.* Duluth MN: Northstar Baptist Ministries, 2001.

Spence, O Talmadge. *The King James Version Case.* Dunn NC: Foundations Bible College, 1981.

Sturz, Harry A. *The Byzantine Text-Type and New Testament Textual Criticism.* Nashville: Thomas Nelson, 1984.

The Authenticity of the Last Twelve Verses of the Gospel According to Mark. London: Trinitarian Bible Society, nd.

The Divine Original. London: Trinitarian Bible Society, nd.

The Scriptural Doctrine of the Holy Trinity. London: Trinitarian Bible Society, 1996.

Thiede, Carsten Peter, and Matthew D'Ancona. *The Jesus Papyrus.* London: Weidenfeld & Nicolson, 1996.

Tow, S H. *Beyond Versions: A Biblical Perspective of Modern English Bibles.* Singapore: King James Productions, 1998.

Tow, Timothy, and Jeffrey Khoo. *A Theology for Every Christian, Book I: Knowing God and His Word.* Singapore: Far Eastern Bible College Press, 1998.

Van Bruggen, Jakob, *The Ancient Text of the New Testament.* Winnipeg: Premier Publishing, 1976.

Van Kleeck, Peter W. *Fundamentalism's Folly?: A Bible Version Debate Case Study.* Grand Rapids: Institute for Biblical Textual Studies, 1998.

Vance, Laurence M. *A Brief History of English Bible Translations.* Pensacola FL: Vance Publications, 1993.

_____. *Archaic Words and the Authorized Version.* Pensacola FL: Vance Publications, 1996.

Waite, D A. *Dean John William Burgon's Confidence in the King James Bible.* Collingswood NJ: Bible For Today, 1995.

_____. *Dean John William Burgon's Vindication of the Last Twelve Verses of Mark.* Collingswood NJ: Bible For Today, nd.

_____. *Defending the King James Bible: A Fourfold Superiority.* Collingswood NJ: Bible For Today, 1992.

_____. *The Defined King James Bible.* Collingswood NJ: Bible For Today, 1998.

_____. *Foes of the King James Bible Refuted.* Collingswood NJ: Bible For Today, 1997.

_____. *Four Reasons for Defending the King James Bible.* Collingswood NJ: Bible For Today, nd.

_____. *Heresies of Westcott and Hort.* Collingswood NJ: Bible For Today, 1979.

_____. *Westcott and Hort's Greek Text Refuted.* Collingswood NJ: Bible For Today, 1996.

Waite Jr, D A. *The Comparative Readability of the Authorized Version.* Collingswood NJ: Bible For Today, 1996.

APPENDIX

BOB JONES UNIVERSITY AND THE KJV: A CRITIQUE OF *FROM THE MIND OF GOD TO THE MIND OF MAN*

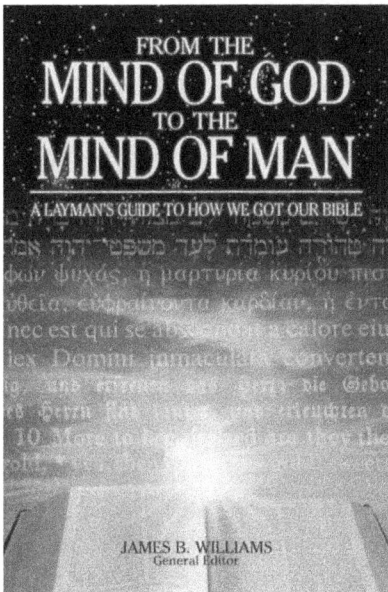

From the Mind of God to the Mind of Man (231 pages)—published in 1999 by Ambassador-Emerald International (Greenville SC, USA, and Belfast, N Ireland), and edited by James B Williams is the latest book to attack KJV-only advocates. KJV-only advocates (1) believe the King James or Authorised Version (KJV/AV) to be the most faithful, trustworthy, and accurate translation of the English Bible available today, and (2) contend that the English-speaking Church should use it alone. A number of books have already been written against the KJV by modernists and neo-evangelicals. *From the Mind of God to the Mind of Man*, however, is written by fundamentalists. Sadly, instead of defending God and His Word, we find fundamentalists singing the same anti-biblical tune of anti-fundamentalists. Sounding like modernists and neoevangelicals, Williams scoffed at KJV-defending fundamentalists, calling them "unqualified," "immature," and a "cancerous sore" (4,7). Is there not treachery within the camp?

James B Williams, the general editor of the book, is on the Bob Jones University (BJU) Board of Trustees. The 19 who contributed to the book are professors, graduates, or friends of BJU. It is reported that Dr Bob Jones III—president of BJU—highly recommended the book in the

1999 World Congress of Fundamentalists, calling it the "most significant book for fundamentalism in this century." It sold like hot cakes. A sad day for fundamentalism it was. By such an endorsement, BJU has kowtowed to the god of humanistic scholarship. *From the Mind of God to the Mind of Man* exalts man's mind over God's. It promotes unregenerate and modernistic scholarship, and downgrades spiritual and biblical discernment.

Now, let us examine the book chapter by chapter.

"Introduction: The Issue We Face" by James B Williams

From the Mind of God to the Mind of Man seeks to address the KJV controversy within fundamentalism. According to Williams, the view that the KJV should be the only translation used by fundamentalists "has created unnecessary confusion and division. ... [and] is doing more damage to the cause of Christ among Fundamentalists than any ... other controversies" (2).

Williams's charge that KJV-only advocates have created "unnecessary confusion and division" is false. The only agenda KJV-only advocates have is to call the Church back to the traditional and preserved text of Scriptures as found in the KJV and its underlying Hebrew and Greek texts over against the plethora of modern and corrupted versions (or perversions) of the Bible. Why should fundamentalists who should be on the Lord's side be angry with those from within their camp who refuse to bow the knee to the modern Baal of Textual Criticism and side with modern Balaams like Westcott and Hort? Williams is upset over the militancy of KJV-only advocates, but is this not what the Lord requires of His Church militant? When false teachers seek to destroy God's Word and His Church, how can God's people not be filled with righteous indignation and speak out passionately in defence of both the Living and Written Word? How can we not be like loyal David who declared, "Do not I hate them, O LORD, that hate thee? and am not I grieved with those that rise up against thee? I hate them with perfect hatred: I count them mine enemies" (Ps 139:21–22)? Westcott and Hort and their cohorts are enemies of Christ and His Word. The prophet Jehu's words to compromising Jehoshaphat apply equally to BJU, "Shouldest thou help the ungodly, and love them that hate the LORD?" (2 Chr 19:1–2). The Bob Jones sanhedrin is telling KJV-only fundamentalists to shut up. But we reply with the Apostle Peter, "We ought to obey God rather than men" (Acts 5:29).

The biblical voice of KJV-only advocates is one and is clear, namely this: We believe and teach that "the Texts which are closest to the original autographs of the Bible are the Traditional Masoretic Hebrew Text for the Old Testament, and the Traditional Greek Text for the New Testament underlying the King James Version." And we believe and teach that

> the King James Version (or Authorised Version) of the English Bible is a true, faithful, and accurate translation of these two providentially preserved Texts (ie, the Traditional Masoretic Hebrew Text and Traditional Greek Text underlying the KJV), which in our time has no equal among all of the other English Translations. The translators did such a fine job in their translation task that we can without apology hold up the Authorised Version of 1611 and say 'This is the Word of God!' while at the same time realising that, in some verses, we must go back to the underlying original language Texts for complete clarity, and also compare Scripture with Scripture (The Dean Burgon Society, Articles of Faith, Section II.A).

Wherein lies the confusion? The confusion is not caused by KJV-only advocates but by fundamentalists who blur the issue by being neutral, claiming to be "balanced" (9). What is BJU's official position on Westcott and Hort, and modern versions? David L Turner in his book—*Standing Without Apology* (BJU Press, 1997)—on the history of BJU wrote,

> The position of the school's Bible Department was especially important. The statement authored by Stewart Custer and Marshall Neal was approved by the entire Bible faculty. ... the department believed "that *the text based upon the Alexandrian manuscripts is, as a whole, superior to the text based upon manuscripts of the Middle Ages.*" ... They concluded the statement by saying, "Christians should be *free to choose* and use either of these texts and still work together in harmony to teach and preach the Word of God to those who are without it."

> In keeping with the University's commitment to balance, it is interesting to note that among the Bob Jones University graduate school Bible faculty, there are some who hold to the superiority of the Majority Text and others who hold to the Westcott and Hort Alexandrian Text. *None of the Bible faculty accepts the Textus Receptus of Erasmus as superior to either the Majority or Alexandrian texts.*

BJU adopts a neutral position on the Bible versions. This yes and no, neither for nor against, both-and equivocation of BJU is the cause of the confusion and division within fundamentalism. Was it not middle-of-the-road neo-evangelicalism that created the confusion that is plaguing Christendom today? In his excellent treatise—*The Tragedy of Compromise*—Ernest Pickering, quoting W B Riley, rightly warned against those "in-betweenites." Sadly, on the KJV issue, Pickering has become an "in-betweenite" himself. He contributed to the confusion by writing a congratulatory preface to this so-called "balanced" (read "compromising") book. John Ashbrook warned others against the dangers of "New Neutralism" in his book by the same title. Like Pickering he too succumbed to the "Neutralism" he so ably exposed by contributing a neutral chapter to a neutral tome. It is this neutral attitude of BJU that is causing the confusion within fundamentalism! Dr Dell Johnson of Pensacola Theological Seminary has rightly called this neutralism and compromise "the leaven in fundamentalism." Our plea to our fellow fundamentalists is one they know well: Be ye not unequally yoked together with Westcott and Hort!

"Our Final Authority: Revelation, Inspiration, Inerrancy, Infallibility, and Authority of the Bible" by Randolph Shaylor

Shaylor has done well to argue for the plenary and verbal inspiration of the Bible (19). He believes the Bible to be absolutely inspired in every detail, and without error in all matters (23). The scriptural texts he quoted as proof are the two classic passages on biblical inspiration: 2 Tim 3:15–16, and 2 Pet 1:21.

However, the shortcoming of Shaylor's chapter is his failure to address the doctrine of biblical preservation. Many KJV-opponents deny the existence of this doctrine. Shaylor did not deny this doctrine, but he does seem confused over what preservation entails. In his brief two-sentenced paragraph on "The Preservation of Revelation," he states his belief that God preserves His Word, then confuses it with the way He does it. Shaylor wrote, "God has made His revelation available to others than those to whom it was immediately given ...." How? "... by preserving His truth in written form" (16). This is a fine statement (though it would have been better if he had cited some proof-texts). God has indeed promised that His Holy Scriptures would not only be presented in all its purity to the Church then, but also to the Church now (Ps 12:6–7). But

Shaylor reveals his confusion over preservation by saying that God "guaranteed the veracity of these writings by using the special method of imparting His truth that we know as inspiration." God did not promise to preserve His Word by means of inspiration! This last statement should be placed under the section on inspiration, not preservation. Inspiration is miraculous, but preservation is providential. Inspiration is a non-repeatable work of God in history; preservation is a continuous work of God throughout history. I would therefore rephrase Shaylor's statement this way, *"God imparted His truth without error in written form by using the special method known as divine inspiration, and guaranteed the veracity of these writings by means of another special method called providential preservation."*

Shaylor's confusion over the twin doctrines of inspiration and preservation is compounded by his erroneous view that God's inspiration of His Word resides only in the autographs (ie, the author's actual scripts), and not the copies (regardless of whether it is a particular manuscript or a group of manuscripts) (22). What Shaylor is trying to tell us is that we can only be absolutely sure that the autographs are infallible and inerrant. Only the autographs are inspired, the copies are not. If what Shaylor says is true, then the Church today is bereft of the inspired Scriptures since we no longer have the autographs, only the copies. *From the Mind of God to the Mind of Man* touts itself as "a layman's guide to how we got our Bible." But its rejection of the doctrine of biblical preservation, telling us that only the autographs are inspired, undermines the layman's confidence in the Bible, and casts doubts in his mind whether he has indeed the pure Word of God. Is not this agnostic view of our Scriptures today a stumbling block to the layman? The Lord's warning applies, "But whoso shall offend one of these little ones which believe in me, it were better for him that a millstone were hanged about his neck, and that he were drowned in the depth of the sea" (Matt 18:6).

Shaylor went on to argue that nowhere does the Bible teach or even imply that the copies of Scripture are inerrantly and infallibly inspired (22). If Shaylor is right, then Jesus is wrong. Jesus testified that the OT Scriptures—the Law and the Prophets—that He had (which were copies and not the autographs) were infallible and inerrant to the jot and tittle, and must all be fulfilled (Matt 5:17–18). Jesus knew full well that His

Word was not only divinely inspired, but also divinely preserved. This is clearly taught in Ps 12:6–7,

> The words of the LORD are pure words: as silver tried in a furnace of earth, purified seven times. Thou shalt keep them, O LORD, thou shalt preserve them from this generation for ever.

Shaylor cites B B Warfield to support his view that inspiration extends only to the original autographs (25). We respect Warfield for his many conservative views, but he was wrong to limit the inspiration of the Bible only to the original autographs; inspiration should extend to the apographs (ie, copies) as well. Dr Edward F Hills, in his book—*The King James Version Defended*—explains why,

> If the doctrine of divine inspiration of the Old and New Testament Scriptures is a true doctrine, the doctrine of the providential preservation of these Scriptures must also be a true doctrine. It must be that down through the centuries God has exercised a special, providential control over the copying of the Scriptures and the preservation and use of the original text have been available to God's people in every age. God must have done this, for if He gave the Scriptures to His Church by inspiration as the perfect and final revelation of his will, then it is obvious that He would not allow this revelation to disappear or undergo any alteration of its fundamental character.

> ... if the doctrines of the *divine inspiration* and *providential preservation* of these Scriptures are true doctrines, then the textual criticism of the New Testament is different from that of the uninspired writings of antiquity. The textual criticism of any book must take into account the conditions under which the original manuscripts were written and also under which the copies of these manuscripts were made and preserved. But if the doctrines of the divine inspiration and providential preservation of the Scriptures are true, then THE ORIGINAL NEW TESTAMENT MANUSCRIPTS WERE WRITTEN UNDER SPECIAL CONDITIONS, UNDER THE INSPIRATION OF GOD, AND THE COPIES WERE MADE AND PRESERVED UNDER SPECIAL CONDITIONS, UNDER THE SINGULAR CARE AND PROVIDENCE OF GOD.

In another book—*Believing Bible Study*—Hills warned,

> If we ignore the providential preservation of the Scriptures and defend the New Testament text in the same way that we defend the texts of other ancient books, then we are following the logic of unbelief. For the special, providential preservation of the holy Scriptures is a *fact* and an important fact. Hence when we ignore this fact and deal with the text of the New Testament as we would with the text of other books, we are behaving as unbelievers behave. We are either denying that the providential preservation of the Scriptures is a

fact, or else we are saying that it is not an important fact, not important enough to be considered when dealing with the New Testament text. But if the providential preservation of the Scriptures is not important, why is the infallible inspiration of the original Scriptures important? If God has not preserved the Scriptures by His special providence, why would He have infallibly inspired them in the first place? And if the Scriptures are not infallibly inspired, how do we know that the Gospel message is true? And if the Gospel message is not true, how do we know that Jesus is the Son of God?

It is a dangerous error therefore to ignore the special, providential preservation of the holy Scriptures and to seek to defend the New Testament text in the same way in which we would defend the texts of other ancient books. For the logic of this unbelieving attitude is likely to lay hold upon us and cast us down into a bottomless pit of uncertainty. ... The Bible teaches us that faith is the foundation of reason. *Through faith we understand* (Heb. 11:3). By faith we lay hold on God as He reveals Himself in the holy Scriptures and make Him the starting point of all our thinking. ...

Like the Protestant Reformers therefore we must take God as the starting point of all our thinking. We must *begin* with God. Very few Christians, however, do this consistently. For example, even when a group of conservative Christian scholars meet for the purpose of defending the Textus Receptus and the King James Version, you will find that some of them want to do this in a rationalistic, naturalistic way. Instead of beginning with God, they wish to begin with facts viewed apart from God, with details concerning the New Testament manuscripts which must be regarded as true (so they think) no matter whether God exists or not. ...

Conservative scholars ... say that they believe in the special, providential preservation of the New Testament text. Most of them really don't though, because, as soon as they say this, they immediately reduce this special providential preservation to the vanishing point in order to make room for the naturalistic theories of Westcott and Hort. As we have seen, some say that the providential preservation of the New Testament means merely that the same "substance of doctrine" is found in all the New Testament documents. Others say that it means that the true reading is always present in at least one of the thousands of extant New Testament manuscripts. And still other scholars say that to them the special, providential preservation of the Scriptures means that the true New Testament text was providentially discovered in the mid-19th century by Tischendorf, Tregelles, and Westcott and Hort after having been lost for 1,500 years.

If you adopt one of these false views of the providential preservation of Scriptures, then you are logically on your way toward the denial of the infallible inspiration of the Scriptures. For if God has preserved the Scriptures so carelessly, why would he have infallibly inspired them in the first place? It is not sufficient therefore merely to say that you believe in the doctrine of the special, providential preservation of holy Scriptures. You must *really* believe this doctrine and allow it to guide your thinking. You must begin with Christ and the Gospel and proceed according to the logic of faith. This will lead you to the Traditional text, the Textus Receptus, and the King James Version, in other words, to the common faith.

Not only was Warfield's definition of biblical inspiration faulty, he was also wrong to promote the destructive textual critical theories of Westcott and Hort. Many fundamentalists have unwittingly imbibed the poison of Westcott and Hort through Warfield. BJU and other fundamentalist schools like Calvary Baptist Theological Seminary, Central Baptist Theological Seminary, Detroit Baptist Theological Seminary, Maranatha Baptist Bible College, Northland Baptist Bible College, and Temple Baptist Seminary (all listed on page iii), have all been infected by the Westcott and Hort leaven.

It will not do for Christians to affirm biblical inspiration, yet at the same time deny biblical preservation. Dr Timothy Tow has rightly said,

> We believe the preservation of Holy Scripture and its Divine inspiration stand in the same position as providence and creation. If Deism teaches a Creator who goes to sleep after creating the world is absurd, to hold to the doctrine of inspiration without preservation is equally illogical. ... Without preservation, all the inspiration, God-breathing into the Scriptures, would be lost. But we have a Bible so pure and powerful in every word and it is so because God has preserved it down through the ages.

We affirm with the Westminster divines that our Old and New Testaments, "being immediately inspired by God, and *by His singular care and providence, kept pure in all ages,* are therefore authentic" (WCF 1:8).

Shaylor concludes his chapter by stating in bold, **"We have the Word of God"** (28). But the question remains, which and where? His idea of inspiration, that only the original autographs are inspired, which we do not have today, has left us without a Bible we can say with utmost confidence, "This is the Word of God, inspired, inerrant, intact." If we follow Shaylor's logic with regard to inspiration, we would not be able to say, "We have the Word of God."

"Canonization and Apocrypha" by Paul W Downey

Downey provides a succinct, factual account of the process of biblical canonisation. However, Downey's chapter is skewed by his comment that the KJV of 1611 "followed the Council of Trent, not the Reformers, in its treatment of the Apocrypha" (45). By so saying, Downey gives the distorted impression that the KJV translators had considered the Apocrypha as part of inspired Scripture. This cannot be further from the truth. It is without question, that the translators accepted these apocryphal books only for their historical value. They in no wise considered them to be inspired Scripture. Alexander McClure, in his book—*The Translators Revived*—gave seven reasons why they rejected the Apocrypha:

1. Not one of them is in the Hebrew language, which was alone used by the inspired historians and poets of the Old Testament.

2. Not one of the writers lays any claim to inspiration.

3. These books were never acknowledged as sacred Scriptures by the Jewish Church, and therefore were never sanctioned by our Lord.

4. They were not allowed a place among the sacred books, during the first four centuries of the Christian Church.

5. They contain fabulous statements, and statements which contradict not only the canonical Scriptures, but themselves; as when, in the two Books of Maccabees, Antiochus Epiphanes is made to die three different deaths in as many different places.

6. It inculcates doctrines at variance with the Bible, such as prayers for the dead and sinless perfection.

7. It teaches immoral practices, such as lying, suicide, assassination and magical incantation.

Downey has thus unfairly portrayed the KJV as a Popish Bible because it included the Apocrypha. He cast a slur against the KJV by saying that the Puritans and Separatists rejected the KJV in favour of the Geneva Bible because the latter excluded the Apocrypha (45–6). But this is not the whole truth. Dr Errol F Rhodes and Dr Liana Lupas who edited *The Translators to the Reader: The Original Preface of the King James Version Revised*—present a more accurate picture

> The books of the Apocrypha were included in the King James Version from the first as a matter of course, as they had been in all versions of the English Bible

from the time of Wycliffe (c. 1384), *including the Calvinist Geneva Bible* of 1560. ... The deliberate omission of the Apocrypha from an English Bible is first noted in the 1640 edition of the Geneva Bible, ... Not until the nineteenth century, however, did the omission of the Apocrypha in Protestant Bibles become normal.

The Protestants in those days were obviously a victim of their times. Although the Apocrypha was found in Reformation Bibles (including the Geneva) since Wycliffe, it is clear that all of the Reformers opposed the Roman Catholic Church, and by the same token, rejected the Apocrypha as spurious. The feelings of the KJV translators, some of whom were Puritans, must necessarily be the same as those who produced the Westminster Confession of Faith (1645). In no uncertain terms, the Westminster divines wrote,

> The books commonly called Apocrypha, not being of divine inspiration, are no part of the canon of the Scripture, and therefore are of no authority in the Church of God, nor to be any otherwise approved, or made use of, than other human writings (WCF 1:3).

It is also significant to note that when it came to translating the Apocrypha, the KJV translators did not care very much for it. Scrivener wrote, "It is well known to Biblical scholars that the Apocrypha received very inadequate attention from the revisers of 1611 and their predecessors, so that whole passages remain unaltered from the racy, spirited, rhythmical, but hasty, loose and most inaccurate version ... made by Coverdale for the Bible of 1536."

What can we say about this book—*From the Mind of God to the Mind*—which aims to present a "balanced" view on the KJV issue? So far, this reviewer gets the sense that instead of presenting a "balanced" view, the writers are bent on finding fault with the KJV.

"Let's Meet the Manuscripts" by Mark Minnick

Minnick, in his chapter, dealt with the so-called science of textual criticism. He goes to great lengths to explain to the layman that textual criticism does not "criticise" the Bible but explains and analyses it (70–98). It ought to be noted that most KJV-only advocates do not dispute the need for constructive textual criticism that is founded on the principles of faith and spiritual discernment. What we are against is humanistic and modernistic textual criticism that seeks to take away God's words from us. Such destructive textual criticism is found in these two infamous modernists—Westcott and Hort—who did not believe in the plenary, verbal inspiration of the Holy Scriptures. Westcott and Hort were translators of the Revised Version (RV). In their translation of 2 Tim 3:16, they questioned the doctrine of biblical inspiration by rendering the verse this way, "Every Scripture inspired of God is also profitable...." By placing the copula "is" after "inspired of God," the clause is made to mean that not all parts of Scripture are inspired of God; only those portions which are inspired are profitable. The KJV translators, on the other hand, correctly placed the copula "is" right after "All Scripture:" "All Scripture is given by inspiration of God, and is profitable...." The KJV leaves no ambiguity whatsoever that all of Scripture is divinely inspired. Westcott and Hort's alteration of the KJV's rendering of 2 Tim 3:16 in the RV evinces their limited inerrancy view of Scripture.

When the RV came out in 1881, Robert L Dabney, was furious over its rendering of 2 Tim 3:16, and wrote a scathing attack against it in the *Southern Presbyterian Review* (July 1881),

> The poisonous suggestion intended is that, among the parts of the "scripture" some are inspired and some are not. Our Bible contains fallible parts! The very doctrine of the Socinian and Rationalist. This treacherous version the revisers (viz, Westcott and Hort) have gratuitously sanctioned!

Indeed as modernists, Westcott and Hort were not fit to handle the Scriptures. They cannot be trusted.

What is indeed strange is that Mark Minnick who quoted Dabney (90–91) cannot see that Westcott and Hort are not friends but enemies of the Bible. Their poisonous fruit reveals their reprobate root. In Matt 7:15–18, Jesus had warned,

> Beware of false prophets, which come to you in sheep's clothing, but inwardly they are ravening wolves. Ye shall know them by their fruits. Do men gather grapes of thorns, or figs of thistles? Even so every good tree bringeth forth good fruit; but a corrupt tree bringeth forth evil fruit. A good tree cannot bring forth evil fruit, neither can a corrupt tree bring forth good fruit.

We would think Minnick—a BJU Bible Professor—would rise up in defence of the faith. Sadly, the opposite is true. He praised Westcott and

Hort and called them "careful" textual critics (85). He adopts Westcott and Hort's destructive textual critical method.

Minnick believes in the Westcott and Hort lie that the difference between their revised Greek text and the traditional Greek text is no more than "a thousandth part of the entire text," which he adds is no more than "one page of my entire Testament" (86). Scrivener's Greek Text published in 1881, and reprinted by the Dean Burgon Society Press in 1999, compared the Textus Receptus with the Westcott and Hort Text. Scrivener's comparison reveals 5,604 places where the Westcott and Hort Greek Text differed from the Textus Receptus. His footnotes show that Westcott and Hort changed a total of 9,970 Greek words either by addition or subtraction. That is almost 50 pages of my entire Testament.

Minnick went on to argue that fundamentalists should view the Westcott and Hort text positively as did C H Spurgeon, G Campbell Morgan, Alexander MacClaren, C I Scofield, H A Ironside and others (87–8). As a fundamentalist, Minnick ought to know that our faith must rest not on man (no matter how conservative they might be) but on the Bible alone. *Sola Scriptura!* Minnick's mention of those great preachers of the past only goes to prove that the leaven of Westcott and Hort's destructive textual criticism had also infected them. The leaven has indeed spread far and wide. "A little leaven leaveneth the whole lump" (Gal 5:9).

The general pro-Westcott-Hort slant in Minnick's chapter is not only seen by what he says, but also what he does not say. The great textual scholar—Dean J W Burgon—who defended the KJV is often neglected or ignored by supporters of the modern versions. Minnick is no exception. Burgon is markedly absent in Minnick's discussion about the text. Who is Dean Burgon? Why should he be taken seriously? I will leave Hills to introduce him to you:

> John William Burgon (1813–1888) became an outstanding English scholar and textual critic. Burgon was born at Smyrna, the son of an English merchant. He studied at London University (1829–1830) and then was engaged for a time in his father's business. In 1841 he returned to his studies, entering Oxford University. He received his BA, MA, and BD degrees from Oxford in the years 1845, 1848, and 1871, respectively. He was elected fellow of Oriel College, Oxford, in 1848. He was appointed Gresham professor of divinity at Oxford in 1867. He became vicar of St Mary's Church, Oxford, in 1863, and he was appointed Dean of Chichester in 1876.

Burgon was no mean theologian, and his preaching was well attended. He was the author of numerous publications, including sermons, tracts, commentaries, and biographies. But as he pressed his studies of the New Testament text, he became best known for his work in the sphere of NT textual criticism.

Burgon's lively literary style could possibly be traced to his early days in Smyrna, Turkey; his mother being a native of that country, and his father an English merchant there. At any rate he developed a warm and enthusiastic nature, not typically English, together with a forthright and honest character which would not allow him to accept pseudo-textual criticism. Being driven by the desire to get to the bottom of the false statements being made by the reigning Critics of his day, Burgon devoted the last 30 years of his life to disprove them. Believing firmly that God had providentially preserved the true text of the New Testament, he set out to discover how the depraved and corrupt readings developed. This required him to travel widely. In 1860, for instance, he traveled to the Vatican Library to personally examine Codex B. And in 1862 he traveled to Mt Sinai to inspect the many manuscripts there. Later he made several tours of European libraries, examining and actually collating NT manuscripts wherever he went. At the same time he was compiling his massive Index of the NT Quotations in the Church Fathers, which is deposited in the British Museum, but never published.

Throughout his life Burgon remained unmarried, and no doubt this had some bearing on the fact that he, as he put it, was willing to spend an entire 13-hour day to establish the authenticity of a single letter of the New Testament Text. His masterly accumulation of evidence first became apparent when he confronted the Critics with his 300-page book—*The Last Twelve Verses of the Gospel According to Saint Mark*—in 1871. His evidence was so complete, and his arguments so unassailable that no one tried to refute this book—either point by point, or in total. When the English Revised Version appeared in 1881, he was asked to review it for the *Quarterly Review*. The result was the printing of his review articles in a book which he entitled, *The Revision Revised*. During all of his active life Burgon was accumulating notes and research data in order to establish what he called *The Traditional Text of the Holy Gospels* as the historically authentic and proven Word of God. After his death in 1888, his long-time friend and co-worker—the Rev Edward Miller—gathered together the Dean's notes and issued the two valuable books entitled, *The Traditional Text of the Holy Gospels*; and *The Causes of the Corruption of the Traditional Text of the Holy Gospels* (both 1896).

Through all these works runs Burgon's fundamental thought, viz, that the textual criticism of the Scriptures must be according to the analogy of faith, and because of this it must be different from the textual criticism of any other book. On this he wrote, "That which distinguishes Sacred Science from every other Science which can be named is that it is Divine, and has to do with a

Book which is inspired, and not to be regarded upon a level with the Books of the East, which are held by their votaries to be sacred. ... Even those principles of Textual Criticism which in the case of profane authors are regarded as fundamental are often out of place here" (*Traditional Text*, 9). In this Burgon was diametrically opposed to the other 19th century critics, notably Westcott and Hort, who stated plainly that textual criticism of the Bible should be handled in the same way as with any other book. But Burgon, who never lost sight of the special providence of God which has presided over the transmission of the New Testament down through the ages, expressly set out to maintain against all opponents that the Church was divinely guided to reject the false readings of the early centuries, and to gradually accept the true text. He denied that he was claiming a perpetual miracle that would keep manuscripts from being depraved at various times, and in various places. But "The Church, in her collective capacity, has nevertheless—as a matter of fact—been perpetually purging herself of those shamefully depraved copies which once everywhere abounded within her pale" (*The Revision Revised*, 334–5). He believed that just as God gradually settled the Canon of the New Testament by weaning His churches from non-canonical books, so He did with the Text also.

Not being willing to dig to the depths that Burgon dug, and not being able to disprove Burgon's facts, his opponents (particularly Westcott and Hort) refused to accept his challenges. They adopted a course of simply portraying Burgon as some kind of Don Quixote who jousted at obstacles too hard for him to understand. Or else they pictured him as too violent in his statements, and thus as if he were a madman, they ignored him. In textual criticism textbooks it has become a tradition to hold Burgon up to ridicule, as if he were an obscurantist who foolishly challenged the "assured results" of modern scholarship. This gross misrepresentation is gradually being exposed by the simple expedient of reproducing Burgon's books. The scholarly, close-reasoned, fact-filled works of Burgon have persuaded many a scholar in this last part of the 20th century that God indeed has not abandoned His words from the day after they came abroad, but has instead guided His children so as to preserve every jot and tittle of His Word. The Traditional Text (or, Byzantine Text, as it is called today) being virtually the same in the manuscripts from the 4th century onward, is proof enough of the doctrine of God's preservation of the Text, according to Burgon's reasoning, and his massive accumulation of evidence.

Dean Burgon had an extremely high view of God's Word. He believed in a 100% inerrant Bible. He said,

The Bible is none other than the voice of Him that sitteth upon the throne. Every book of it, every chapter of it, every verse of it, every word of it, every syllable of it, every letter of it, is the direct utterance of the Most High. The Bible is none other than the Word of God, not some part of it more, some part of it less, but all alike the utterance of Him that sitteth upon the throne, faultless, unerring, supreme.

At every annual convocation, the faculty of the Far Eastern Bible College take an oath of allegiance to the Holy Scriptures based on Burgon's words. Whose side are you on? Burgon or Westcott and Hort? If you are on the Lord's side, you would support the former and not the latter.

Minnick lacked discernment and wisdom when he labeled KJV-only advocates "unscripturally divisive" (98). He then reassured his readers that the poisoned waters of Westcott and Hort are safe. He believes the corrupt Westcott and Hort text is superior to the Textus Receptus, and quoting Scofield, condescendingly said that Westcott and Hort "have cleared the Greek Textus Receptus of minor inaccuracies" (96). He also believes that the older but corrupt Alexandrian or Minority Text is to be valued and preferred over the readings of the Majority Text (96).

Is the Alexandrian or Minority Text that good? Dean Burgon in his 550-page magnum opus—*The Revision Revised*—has convincingly proven that the Alexandrian manuscripts of Westcott and Hort are among the most corrupt copies of the New Testament in existence. He said that the Codex Sinaiticus and Codex Vaticanus are

> most scandalously corrupt copies extant:—exhibit the most shamefully mutilated texts which are anywhere to be met with:—have become ... the depositories of the largest amount of fabricated readings, ancient blunders, and intentional perversions of Truth,—which are discoverable in any known copies of the Word of God.

It is significant to note that those two codices run against the readings of the majority (99%) of Greek New Testament manuscripts (over 5000) we have today. To prove the point, let me just cite one example from Dean Burgon to show how corrupt the 5 uncials—Sinaiticus (ℵ), Alexandrinus (A), Vaticanus (B), Ephraemi Rescriptus (C), and Bezae Cantabrigiensis (D)—Westcott and Hort deemed most reliable really are. The passage under consideration is the Lord's Prayer in Luke 11:2–4. The findings of Burgon are as follows:

1. D inserts Matt 6:7, "Use not vain repetitions as the rest: for some suppose that they shall be heard by their much speaking. But when ye pray ...".

2. B and ℵ removed 5 words "Our," and "which art in heaven."

3. D omits the definite article "the" before "name," adds "upon us," and rearranges "Thy Kingdom."

4. B removes the clause, "Thy will be done, as in heaven, also on the earth." Interestingly, ℵ retains these words, but adds "so" before "also," and omits the article before "earth" agreeing for once with A, C, and D.

5. ℵ and D changed the form of the Greek word for "give."

6. ℵ omits definite article before "day by day."

7. D, instead of the 3 last-named words, writes "this day" (from Matt), substitutes "debts" for "sins" (also from Matt), and in place of "for we ourselves" writes "as also we" (again from Matt).

8. ℵ shows great sympathy with D by accepting two-thirds of this last blunder, exhibiting "as also [we] ourselves."

9. D consistently read "our debtors" in place of "every one that is indebted to us."

10. B and ℵ canceled the last petition "but deliver us from evil," going against A, C, and D.

Dean Burgon astutely judged,

So then, these five 'first-class authorities' are found to throw themselves into *six different combinations* in their departures from S. Luke's way of exhibiting the Lord's Prayer,—which, among them, they contrive to falsify in respect of no less than 45 words; and yet *they are never able to agree among themselves as to any single various reading*: while *only once* are more than two of them observed to stand together,—viz. in the unauthorized omission of the article. In respect of 32 (out of the 45) words, *they bear in turn solitary evidence*. What need to declare that it is *certainly false* in every instance? Such however is the infatuation of the Critics, that the vagaries of B are all taken for gospel. Besides omitting the 11 words which B omits jointly with ℵ, Drs. Westcott and Hort erase from the Book of Life those other 11 precious words which are omitted by B only. And in this way it comes to pass that the mutilated condition to which the scalpel of Marcion the heretic reduced the Lord's Prayer some 1730 years ago, (for mischief can all be traced back to *him!*), is palmed off on the Church of England by the Revisionists as the work of the Holy Ghost!

So what is the bottom line? Should fundamentalists use the Westcott and Hort text and method? Our BJU friends should listen to Dr Alfred Martin, former Vice-President of Moody Bible Institute:

The only road to progress in New Testament textual criticism is repudiation of their (ie, Westcott and Hort) theory and all its fruits. Most contemporary criticism is bankrupt and confused, the result of its liaison with liberal theology. A Bible-believing Christian can never be content to follow the leadership of those who do not recognize the Bible as the verbally inspired Word of God. The Textus Receptus is the starting-point for future research, because it embodies substantially and in a convenient form the traditional text.

"The History of the Textus Receptus" by John E Ashbrook

Ashbrook's chapter employs a "soothe then slap" approach to evaluating the Textus Receptus, and its first editor—Erasmus. Ashbrook begins by praising Erasmus for his genius as a biblical and textual scholar, and then castigates him as a modernist (102). It is very careless of KJV critics to label Erasmus a modernist. Erasmus, like Luther, had his doctrinal weaknesses, but he was hardly a modernist. Modernists like Westcott and Hort have a very low view of Scripture. Erasmus on the other hand had a high view of Scripture evinced by his painstakingly edited Greek New Testament which in no small way aided the cause of the Reformation. Like the Reformers, Erasmus desired the Scriptures to be translated into all languages so that every one could read it and know Christ for himself. Hear his testimony:

> I would have the weakest woman read the Gospels and the Epistles of St. Paul ... I would have those words translated into all languages, so that not only Scots and Irishmen, but Turks and Saracens might read them. I long for the plowboy to sing them to himself as he follows the plow, ... Other studies we may regret having undertaken, but happy is the man upon whom death comes when he is engaged in these. These sacred words give you the very image of Christ speaking, healing, dying, rising again, and make Him so present, that were He before your very eyes you would not more truly see Him.

Ashbrook disparagingly says that Erasmus was "a loyal son of the Catholic Church" (102). This is another misrepresentation. Erasmus publicly exposed the heresies and superstitions of the Roman Catholic Church. This angered the pope so much that he branded Erasmus "an impious heretic," and banned his books from being read by Catholics. The pope evidently was able to see that Erasmus was a Reformer at heart. However, as a Reformer, Erasmus's main fault was in his failure to separate from the false Catholic Church (cf 2 Cor 6:14–7:1). Luther succeeded in his reformation because he did it from without, but Erasmus failed because he chose to do it from within. Nevertheless, as someone had observed, it was Erasmus who laid the egg of the Reformation, and Luther was left to hatch it.

Ashbrook is unhappy with people who scoff at Westcott and Hort just because they were textual critics (104, 108). He contends that KJV advocates who reject Westcott and Hort as textual critics, must likewise reject Erasmus for he too was a textual critic. We do not dispute that Erasmus did the work of textual criticism, but the question is not on textual criticism per se, but the type of textual criticism employed. Westcott and Hort invented a textual critical method which sought to take God's Word away from God's people. The amount of verses Westcott and Hort scissored out from our Bible is equivalent to that of First and Second Peter. Erasmus, on the other hand, did not engage in this type of deconstructive textual criticism. Erasmus's textual critical work was guided by the common faith, ie, the belief that God had providentially preserved the Scriptures down through the ages. Edward F Hills said,

> In the days of Erasmus, … it was commonly believed by well informed Christians that the original New Testament text had been providentially preserved in the current New Testament text, primarily in the current Greek text and secondarily in the current Latin text. Erasmus was influenced by this common faith and probably shared it, and God used it providentially to guide Erasmus in his editorial labors on the Textus Receptus.

What sets Erasmus apart from Westcott and Hort was his belief that God has kept His Word intact down through the centuries. This caused him to edit the Greek New Testament with great reverence, taking care not to snip away God's Word. Westcott and Hort's textual critical work was quite different. Both denied the doctrines of inspiration and preservation, and thus had no qualms whatsoever in spurning the majority of New Testament Scripture that God had preserved for His people down through the ages in favour of two extremely corrupted texts which the Church had already seen fit to discard.

If Erasmus was such a faithful textual critic, then how would one explain the charge that in his hurry to complete his Greek text, he translated the last few verses of Revelation from Latin to Greek because the last page of his manuscript on Revelation was missing? Hills gave another side to this,

The last six verses of Codex 1r (Rev. 22:16–21) were lacking, ... According to almost all scholars, Erasmus endeavoured to supply these deficiencies in his manuscript by retranslating the Latin Vulgate into Greek. Hoskier, however, was inclined to dispute this on the evidence of manuscript 141. In his 4ᵗʰ edition of his Greek New Testament (1527) Erasmus corrected much of this translation Greek (if it was indeed such) on the basis of a comparison with the Complutensian Polyglot Bible ...

It is customary for naturalistic critics to make the most of human imperfections in the Textus Receptus and to sneer at it as a mean and almost sordid thing. ... But those who concentrate in this way on the human factors involved in the production of the Textus Receptus are utterly unmindful of the Providence of God. For in the very next year, in the plan of God, the Reformation was to break out in Wittenberg, and it was important that the Greek New Testament should be published first in one of the future strongholds of Protestantism by a book seller who was eager to place it in the hands of the people and not in Spain, the land of the Inquisition, by the Roman Church, which was intent on keeping the Bible from the people.

Ashbrook is right to observe that the view of biblical preservation "must be accepted by faith," but wrong to say that this faith is based on "human assumption" (106). This belief on biblical preservation is based not on human assumption but divine revelation (Exod 32:15–19, 34:1–4, Pss 12:6–7, 78:1–8, 105:8, 119:89,111,152,160, Prov 22:20–21, Eccl 3:14, Jer 36:30–32, Matt 4:4, 5:17–18, 24:35, John 10:35, Col 1:17, 1 Pet 1:23–25, Rev 22:18–19).

"Printed Greek Texts" by William H Smallman

Smallman's chapter presents a succinct update on the history of the printed Greek texts. However, in his evaluation of the two distinct families of printed Greek texts, viz, the Minority/Westcott-Hort/Critical text, and the Majority/Textus Receptus/Traditional text, it is unfortunate that he favours the so-called "eclectic" text or "balanced" approach which is essentially pro-Westcott and Hort.

In his opening discussion, Smallman says that the first printed Greek text (which became the Textus Receptus) by Erasmus was "hastily edited," and that he used only "half dozen or so manuscripts" (169–70). This invariably gives the layman the impression that the Textus Receptus was a result of sloppy work. Is this an accurate portrayal of Erasmus and his work? Hills rose to Erasmus' defence,

By his travels [Erasmus] was brought into contact with all the intellectual currents of his time and stimulated to almost superhuman efforts. He became the most famous scholar and author of his day and one of the most prolific writers of all time, his collected works filling ten large volumes .... As an editor also his productivity was tremendous. Ten columns of the catalogue of the library in the British Museum are taken up with the bare enumeration of the works translated, edited, or annotated by Erasmus, and their subsequent reprints. Included are the greatest names of the classical and patristic world, such as Ambrose, Aristotle, Augustine, Basil, Chrysostom, Cicero, and Jerome. An almost unbelievable showing.

To conclude, there was no man in all Europe better prepared than Erasmus for the work of editing the first printed Greek New Testament text, and this is why, we may well believe, God chose him and directed him providentially in the accomplishment of this task.

Did Erasmus employ other manuscripts besides those five he had when preparing his Greek text? Hills answered,

The indications are that he did. ... It is well known also that Erasmus looked for manuscripts everywhere during his travels and that he borrowed them from everyone he could. Hence although the Textus Receptus was based mainly on the manuscripts which Erasmus found at Basel, it also included readings taken from others to which he had access. It agreed with the common faith because it was founded on manuscripts which in the providence of God were readily available.

To those who sought to demean Erasmus and the Textus Receptus, Dean Burgon had this to say, "to describe the haste with which Erasmus produced the first published edition of the NT, to make sport about the copies which he employed, all this kind of thing is the preceding of one who seeks to mislead his readers to throw dust in their eyes, to divert their attention from the problems actually before them." I cannot agree more.

When it came for Smallman to describe the Westcott and Hort text, he called it "an important development," and hailed the Codex Sinaiticus as "one of the finest quality manuscripts" in existence (172). He said that the Westcott and Hort text "produced a revolution," which led to "a new quest to define the original text," to be "based on new witnesses ... and on new approaches to interpreting the variants." He also noted that the Westcott and Hort text and its offshoots contain "significant differences" from the Textus Receptus (171). Were those differences for the better or for the worse? Are the verses removed from the Textus Receptus by Westcott and Hort authentic or spurious? Smallman in his attempt to maintain his balancing act refused to say or commit himself. He wrote evasively, "It is not the purpose of this essay to debate the fundamentals of Wescott [sic] and Hort's principles and canons" (173).

Smallman considers the modern, critical Greek texts of Nestle and Aland (NA), and the United Bible Societies (UBS) to be the "Standard Greek Testament." He said, "The establishment of the United Bible Societies/Nestle-Aland Text as standard is accepted by many virtually without argument" (179). He also says that this "Standard Greek Text" "has been achieved by the majority of textual scholars who prefer the minority of manuscripts" (179). Despite the fact that this so-called "Standard Greek Text" is based only on a "minority of the manuscripts" (ie, the corrupt Alexandrian manuscripts), Smallman has interestingly nothing negative to say about it. Like the modernists and neo-evangelicals, he takes the eclectic view that the critical UBS and NA Greek texts are truly "scholarly" and "balanced" vis-a-vis the Textus Receptus.

Are the UBS and NA Greek texts truly eclectic (ie, a mixture of all available texts), or are they really the Westcott and Hort text disguised; a wolf in sheep's clothing? According to Radmacher and Hodges, the new "Textus Receptus" of the UBS and NA "do not differ a whole lot from the text produced by Westcott-Hort in 1881." Gordon Fee, who is no fundamentalist, also acknowledged, "[In] Modern textual criticism, the 'eclecticism' of the UBS, RSV, NIV, NASB etc., ... recognizes that Westcott-Hort's view of things was essentially correct." Thus the term "eclectic" is but a smokescreen.

The UBS Greek Text itself when it first came out acknowledged that its work was carried out "on the basis of Westcott and Hort's edition of the Greek New Testament." It is thus no surprise that the first two editions of the UBS text relegated the *pericope de adultera* (John 7:53–8:11) from its original and traditional place to the end of the Gospel; this to show that the passage is considered non-authentic. This clearly reveals a Westcott and Hort attitude. Like Westcott and Hort, the UBS editors accepted without question the omission of those verses in the corrupt Alexandrian manuscripts over against the Traditional and Majority Text.

It is interesting to note that the third edition transposed John 7:53–8:11 back to its original location. Are the editors now admitting their error in rejecting the pericope? Although the pericope is now returned to its rightful place, the passage is enclosed by double brackets. What do these double brackets mean? The UBS editors say, "Double brackets in the text indicate that the enclosed passages which are usually rather extensive are known not to be a part of the original text." Not only this precious passage, but also Mark's last 12 verses are also assigned double brackets. The UBS editors would like us to know that both passages are not inspired Scripture. Do you not see the forked tongue of the snake here? Why are fundamentalists hissing to the same tune? Are the last 12 verses of Mark, the *pericope de adultera* (John 7:53–8:11), the Johannine Comma (1 John 5:7), and a host of other verses Westcott and Hort removed from the Textus Receptus, divinely inspired? If you are looking to Smallman for answers, look no more! He is so "balanced," he leaves you clueless.

Smallman would neither debate nor examine Westcott and Hort, but would spend three full pages (172–5) explaining their textual critical method which he deemed "profitable" (173), as compared to only half a page for the Textus Receptus (180). Do you not see the bias? Dean Burgon was only given cursory mention. Smallman did not consider Burgon's books in defence of the Textus Receptus and KJV to be worth his time. Yet, Smallman was quick to use Burgon when it came time to undermine the layman's confidence in the KJV. He quoted Burgon as saying,

> Once for all, we request it may be clearly understood that we do not, by any means, claim perfection for the Received Text. We entertain no extravagant notions on this subject. Again and again we shall have occasion to point out ... that the Textus Receptus needs correction (182).

But Smallman should not have stopped there, giving a skewed picture. Burgon went on to express how deeply he appreciated the Textus Receptus,

> We do but insist, (1) That it is an incomparably better text than that which either Lachmann, Tischendorf, or Tregelles has produced: infinitely preferable to the 'New Greek Text' of the Revisionists (viz, Westcott and Hort). And, (2) That to be improved, the Textus Receptus will have to be revised on entirely different 'principles' from those which are just now in fashion. Men must begin by unlearning the *German (ie, liberal) prejudices* ... and address themselves, instead to the stern logic of *facts*.

In his conclusion, Smallman reveals his confusion. He wrote quite rightly that

> The divine preservation of the Scriptures is a fact that gives great assurance to those who read the Bible today. It is the Word of God, and every "jot and tittle" of it is kept intact for the readers of successive generations (182).

But in the next sentence he turns agnostic: "Still, our certainty of the preservation of the text does not identify which text family is the object of that providential oversight." To him, the text is preserved in all the texts whether corrupt or not. Such a position is clearly illogical, and contradictory. I would urge readers to listen to Hills instead of Smallman, Let me repeat Hills' most pertinent warning here,

> It is a dangerous error therefore to ignore the special, providential preservation of the holy Scriptures and to seek to defend the New Testament text in the same way in which we would defend the texts of other ancient books. For the logic of this unbelieving attitude is likely to lay hold upon us and cast us down into a bottomless pit of uncertainty. ...

> The Bible teaches us that faith is the foundation of reason. *Through faith we understand* (Heb. 11:3). By faith we lay hold on God as He reveals Himself in the holy Scriptures and make Him the starting point of all our thinking. ...

> Like the Protestant Reformers therefore we must take God as the starting point of all our thinking. We must begin with God. Very few Christians, however, do this consistently. For example, even when a group of conservative Christian scholars meet for the purpose of defending the Textus Receptus and the King James Version, you will find that some of them want to do this in a rationalistic, naturalistic way. Instead of beginning with God, they wish to begin with facts viewed apart from God, with details concerning the New Testament manuscripts which must be regarded as true (so they think) no matter whether God exists or not. ...

> Conservative scholars ... say that they believe in the special, providential preservation of the New Testament text. Most of them really don't though, because, as soon as they say this, they immediately reduce this special providential preservation to the vanishing point in order to make room for the naturalistic theories of Westcott and Hort. As we have seen, some say that the providential preservation of the New Testament means merely that the same "substance of doctrine" is found in all the New Testament documents. Others say that it means that the true reading is always present in at least one of the thousands of extant New Testament manuscripts. And still other scholars say that to them the special, providential preservation of the Scriptures means that the true New Testament text was providentially

discovered in the mid-19th century by Tischendorf, Tregelles, and Westcott and Hort after having been lost for 1,500 years.

If you adopt one of these false views of the providential preservation of Scriptures, then you are logically on your way toward the denial of the infallible inspiration of the Scriptures. For if God has preserved the Scriptures so carelessly, why would he have infallibly inspired them in the first place? It is not sufficient therefore merely to say that you believe in the doctrine of the special, providential preservation of holy Scriptures. You must *really* believe this doctrine and allow it to guide your thinking. You must begin with Christ and the Gospel and proceed according to the logic of faith. This will lead you to the Traditional text, the Textus Receptus, and the King James Version, in other words, to the common faith.

Can we be certain of God's Word? God in Prov 22:20–21 says, "Have not I written to thee excellent things in counsels and knowledge, That I might make thee know *the certainty of the words of truth*; that thou mightest answer the words of truth to them that send unto thee?" Be sure of this: God wants us to have certainty concerning His Words.

"The Making of the King James Version" by John C Mincy

Despite its helpful historical data, this chapter misrepresents the KJV translators in a most misleading way. In support of modern and corrupt versions, Mincy argued that the KJV translators themselves "viewed even the worst English versions as the Word of God" (141). He quoted them as saying, "Now to answer our enemies; we do not deny, rather we affirm and insist that the very worst translation of the Bible in English issued by Protestants contains the word of God, or rather, is the word of God." This statement is most illogical and totally unbiblical!

Were the KJV translators capable of those words; the ones who extolled truth and condemned error? Consider what they wrote in their preface—"The Translators to the Readers,"

> But now what piety without truth? What truth (what saving truth) without the word of God? What word of God (whereof we may be sure) without the Scripture? The Scriptures we are commanded to search (John 5.39; Isaiah 8.20). They are reproved that were unskilful in them, or slow to believe them (Matthew 22.29; Luke 24.25). They can make us wise unto salvation (2 Timothy 3.15). If we be ignorant, they will instruct us; if out of the way, they will bring us home; if out of order, they will reform us; if in heaviness, comfort us; if dull, quicken us; if cold, inflame us. *Tolle, lege, Tolle, lege*, Take up and read, take up

and read the Scriptures ... The Scriptures then being acknowledged to be so full and so perfect, how can we excuse ourselves of negligence, if we do not study them? ... It is not only an armor, but also a whole armory of weapons, both offensive and defensive; whereby we may save ourselves and put the enemy to flight. It is not an herb, but a tree, or rather a whole paradise of trees of life, which bring forth fruit every month, and the fruit thereof is for meat, and the leaves for medicine. It is not a pot of Manna, or a cruse of oil, which were for memory only, or for a meal's meat or two; but as it were a shower of heavenly bread sufficient for a whole host, be it never so great, and as it were a whole cellar full of oil vessels; whereby all our necessities may be provided for, and our debts discharged. In a word, it is a panary of wholesome food, against fenowed traditions; a physician's shop ... of preservatives against poisoned heresies; a pandect of profitable laws against rebellious spirits; a treasury of most costly jewels against beggarly rudiments; finally, a fountain of most pure water springing up unto everlasting life. ... Happy is the man that delighteth in the Scripture, and thrice happy that meditateth in it day and night.

Could the men who penned the above words have sanctioned a corrupt translation of the Scriptures? Would they have cried, *Tolle, lege, Tolle, lege,* if John 1:29 had read thus, "Behold the *Pig* of God, which taketh away the sin of the world?" If the "fountain of most pure water" had been polluted by enemies of the Word in such a way, I am quite certain that the KJV translators would have cursed that version for blasphemy, and cast it into the fire. It is truly absurd for Mincy to think that the KJV translators humoured wicked versions. Indeed the Puritans among the KJV translators appealed to the king for a new English Bible because the Bible as found in the Communion book was according to them, "a most corrupted translation." Evidently, corrupt translations did not sit well with them at all.

The question remains: Did the KJV translators really say that the "worst" versions are acceptable? They certainly did not. Mincy's quotation of the KJV translators is taken from Rhodes and Lupas's *paraphrase* (published by the American Bible Society in 1997) of their original statement. It is obvious that Rhodes and Lupas felt quite free to change the original intent of those words, taking them out of context. How did the original version read especially in context?

Now to the latter we answer, that we do not deny, nay, we affirm and avow, that the very *meanest* translation of the Bible in English set forth by men of our profession (for we have seen none of theirs of the whole Bible as yet) containeth the word of God, nay, is the word of God: as the King's speech which he uttered in parliament, being translated into French, Dutch, Italian, and Latin, is still the King's speech, though it be not interpreted by every translator *with the like grace, ...*

It is clear that by the word "meanest" they did not mean "worst" (ie, "evil in the highest degree"). Who would dare mistranslate the king's speech? Clearly they were not talking about sense but *style*. By "meanest" they meant *poor in literary grace*. When beginning Greek students translate their Greek Bible into English, it may be rough and wooden; but if literal and precise, it is the Word of God.

"The Changing King James Version," by Mark R Simmons

In this chapter, Simmons ridicules KJV-only advocates by setting up a straw man. He calls KJV-only advocates overly simplistic for believing that the actual "1611" KJV is the "preserved" Word of God (161). Of course, no right thinking KJV defender would say that. First, KJV-only advocates believe that the preserved text is the Hebrew and Greek text that underlies the KJV. The Masoretic Hebrew Old Testament (Ben Chayyim edition, 1524–5), and the Greek Textus Receptus (Beza's 5th edition, 1598) on which the KJV is based are the preserved Old Testament, and New Testament text respectively. Second, when KJV defenders say they uphold the KJV of 1611, they do not mean the exact 1611 edition. KJV defenders like their detractors know that the KJV currently in print is the 1769 edition. The KJV was originally published in the year 1611. To identify certain things by their year of origination is common practice. For example, Biblical Theological Seminary was founded in the year 1971. It was not known as "Biblical Theological Seminary" at that time but "Biblical School of Theology." When there was a name change in 1978, did the school also change its year of establishment? Of course not! It remained 1971. Likewise, to refer to the present edition of the KJV as the KJV of 1611 is neither unusual, nor deceptive; it simply reflects history.

Simmons exaggerates when he says that the KJV is "extremely difficult" to understand because "over four thousand words in the King James Bible are not found in even the best of our one volume English dictionaries today" (153). There are just about 200 archaic words in the

KJV, and most of these words can be found in our Webster's, Oxford, and Chambers dictionaries. The recently published *Defined King James Bible*, edited by Dr D A Waite and his son, has footnoted the modern meaning of all archaic words in the KJV. There is really no excuse now not to use the KJV just because some of its words are archaic.

Anti-KJVists often ridicule the use of the "thees" and "thous" in the KJV, simply because these archaic pronouns are no longer common today. But is this a good reason to abandon the KJV? In an article entitled, "Is a Pronominal Revision of the Authorised Version Desirable?," Dr Oswald T Allis wrote,

> It is a well-known fact that in contemporary English the forms *thou, thy, thine* have almost disappeared from secular use. They are largely restricted to the language of religious devotion, in which they are constantly employed, and which is largely formed by, and owes its peculiarities to, the Authorised Version. Consequently, it is often asserted or assumed that the usage of the AV represents the speech of 300 years ago, and that now, three centuries later, it should be changed to accord with contemporary usage. But this is not at all a correct statement of the problem. The important fact is this. The usage of the AV is *not* the ordinary usage of the early seventeenth century: it *is* the Biblical usage based on the style of the Hebrew and Greek Scriptures. The second part of this statement needs no proof and will be challenged by no one. It is undeniable that where the Hebrew and Greek use the singular of the pronoun the AV regularly uses the singular, and where they use the plural it uses the plural. Even in Deuteronomy where in his addresses, and apparently for rhetorical and pedagogical effect, Moses often changes suddenly, and seemingly arbitrarily, from singular to plural or from plural to singular, the AV reproduces the style of the text with fidelity. That is to say, the usage of the AV is *strictly Biblical*.

If the fundamentalists who wrote *From the Mind of God to the Mind of Man* believe in verbal inspiration, they should be quick to defend the use of the "archaic" pronouns of the KJV which accurately render in English the singular and plural pronouns of the Hebrew and Greek Scriptures. It would indeed be a contradiction in faith and practice for them to consider the "thees" and the "thous" to be unimportant and insignificant.

Simmons also makes a big deal out of the many revisions of the KJV (156–165). The KJV of 1611 went through a number of revisions soon after publication but all of which were completed in 1629. The revisions that occurred between 1611 and 1629 were due to printing errors. These errors were corrected by the KJV translators themselves, namely Samuel Ward and John Bois. In the course of typesetting, the printers had inadvertently left out words or phrases; all such typographical errors were corrected. Another revision of the KJV was done between 1762 and 1769. This revision had to do with spelling. For example, old forms which had an "e" after verbs, and "u" instead of "v," and "f" for "s" were all standardised to conform to modern spelling. For example, "feare" is "fear," "mooued" is "moved," and "euill" is "evil," and "alfo," is "also." All these Gothic and German spelling peculiarities have been Romanised by 1769. It is important to note that the 1769 edition is essentially the same as the 1611.

"English Versions Since 1880," by J Drew Conley

Conley in his article cast KJV-only advocates in a bad light. Quoting the KJV translators who said that the Bible should be translated into the language of the common man, he obliquely accused those who insist that the "archaic" KJV alone is the acceptable English Bible for hiding God's Word from people just like the Romanists in days gone by (187–9). Conley argues that the profound changes in English since the 1600s has caused many words in the KJV to

> come up blank in the reader's thinking—or worse, misunderstood ... And when the text is the Bible, lack of understanding does spiritual harm. ... For me to expect members of the congregation—especially new converts— to devote themselves to profitable study of a Bible in an unfamiliar language is certainly wishful thinking at best" (183).

Conley's concern over the "understandability" of the KJV is well taken, but his solution to the difficulty is a step backwards, not forwards. For young believers, it is not just the archaisms in the Bible that may pose some difficulty, but also the many hard theological terms. How should the pastor advise the young believer? Use the NIV, or TEV, or CEV, or RSV, or NASB, or the Living Bible? This would be like giving a baby milk laced with arsenic! Conley rightly says that the pastor has a duty "to communicate God's truth so others understand" (192). He continues,

> There are words of such great theological significance that they should never be replaced. A preacher should define them, explain them, and illustrate them so that others can make them their own. *Justification, sanctification, glorification, propitiation, atonement, reconciliation,* understood by few except those who have

been taught the gospel, have been too precisely defined over the years to abandon them without grave consequences" (192).

If pastors have a duty to explain all those important theological terms to their congregation so that they might understand, why cannot they do the same for the archaic words in the KJV? Furthermore, why cannot the young believer be taught to use the dictionary to locate the meaning of those words, or better still, why cannot the pastor present to him a copy of *The Defined King James Bible*? Why should the young Christian be told to throw out his KJV and get an NIV or some other perversion of the Bible just because of some old words?

The excuse not to use the KJV because it contains archaic words is really quite flimsy. When we read a modern book, do we not find words that we do not understand? When we encounter such difficulties in our reading, what do we do? Throw the book away? or hit the dictionary? We go to the dictionary. We search for the meaning, and we become the wiser for it. We are not fools are we? Why should God's Word in the KJV be treated so disrespectfully, that when we come across difficult terms, it is beneath us to turn the dictionary? Should modern English versions be preferred over the KJV? Dr Robert B Alter (PhD, Harvard) in 1996, wrote, "Modern English versions put readers at a grostesque distance from the ... Bible. To this day, the Authorized Version of 1611 (the "King James Bible") ... for all its archaisms ... remains the closest we have yet come to the distinctive experience of the original." Therefore, stick to the KJV, and use the dictionary!

The neo-evangelical spirit that pervades this book—*From the Mind of God to the Mind of Man*—is clearly seen in Conley's approach to the versions. One would think Conley, a fundamentalist pastor, would be careful to guide his sheep to the right pasture with regard to the versions. Instead, we find him saying that his chapter is not "intended to be a critique or a recommendation of any version" (195). He will not tell the layman (and mind you, this book is supposed to be a guide for the layman) which version is good and which is bad. As God's undershepherd, he is telling the Lord's sheep, "There are weeds, thistles, and grass out there. I do not wish to tell you where to go, or what to eat; just go take your pick." But wait, Conley does not do even that. In a footnote, he recommends the following versions which he says "are valuable for serious Bible study" (195): the Revised Version, American Standard Version and the New American Standard Bible (NASB). Note that all three are based on the corrupt text of Westcott and Hort. In a whisper, he tells the sheep, "Go eat the weeds and the thistles." It is thus no surprise that Conley writes sympathetically of the liberal and ecumenical Revised Standard Version (RSV). He quotes without any refutation that the RSV embodies "the best results of modern scholarship" (198). He quotes the RSV as saying that the KJV has "grave defects" without any rebuttal whatsoever, except for a cowardly parenthetical remark, "their words, not mine" (198).

What is truly troubling is Conley's tacit approval of the RSV's heterodox translation of the עלמה (*almah*) of Isa 7:14 as "young woman" instead of "virgin" (199). He justifies the RSV by pointing out that Matthew's quotation of Isa 7:14 in the RSV reads "virgin." Why did Conley not defend the orthodox translation of Isa 7:14 as found in the KJV over against the RSV? Perhaps Conley holds to the neo-evangelical view that Isa 7:14 has two fulfilments: one in the time of Isaiah, and the other in the time of Christ. If Conley does allow for such a translation and interpretation of Isa 7:14, he is no fundamentalist. It is well known that in 1952, when the RSV was released, fundamentalist scholars took the RSV to task for its heretical treatment of Isa 7:14. Conley must surely know this, yet he does not seem to care.

If Conley is sympathetic to the RSV, he is enthusiastic about the NASB. He says the NASB

> incorporates the *gains* made by the discoveries of additional manuscripts (ie, Alexandrian manuscripts) ... and has thus proven of *great value* in discerning the underlying text. To some its strength carries with it a weakness—that of falling short of a smooth English style. Others fault it, along with almost all the modern versions for the Greek textual family it uses. Neither charge is totally fair to this *excellent* tool for Bible study" (201).

Conley tells his readers that he will neither recommend nor critique, but does not his remarks about the NASB sound like a recommendation? The layman would do well to note that the NASB, though rather literal, is unreliable because it is based on the corrupt Westcott and Hort text.

If the layman wants to find guidance on which English versions are reliable and which are not, he would do well to skip Conley, and find it somewhere else. One good source is *A Brief History of English Bible Translations* by Laurence M Vance.

"Conclusion: The Response to These Facts," by Keith E Gephart

Gephart reiterates the aim of the book which is to fault certain fundamentalists for taking a pro-KJV or KJV-only position. He says, "As always, Fundamentalism's greatest difficulties are caused by those within its own ranks who by some actions, statements, or doctrinal positions bring embarassment and unnecessary discord" (211). Such rhetoric is no different from that of Ahab to Elijah, "Art thou he that troubleth Israel?" (1 Kgs 18:17)." Like Elijah we reply, "I have not troubled Israel; but thou, and thy father's house, in that ye have forsaken the commandments of the LORD, and thou hast followed Baalim" (1 Kgs 18:18). KJV-only advocates have been faithful to the Hebrew and Greek texts God has inspired and preserved down through the ages. Pan-Versionists like Gephart have shunted from the traditional and preserved text to embrace the modernist and critical text of Westcott and Hort, the UBS, and NA. The old, conservative textual line began in the time of the Apostles, and preserved all through the centuries by God, culminating in the Textus Receptus of the 16th century Reformation. This line continued until Satan introduced a new, modernistic line in the Westcott and Hort text of 19th century liberalism. Know that the 19th century was a time of great unbelief when new-fangled "isms" like Evolutionism, Liberalism, Freudianism, Marxism, and Ecumenism came into being. It looks like modern fundamentalists instead of traveling on the "good old gospel train," have hopped onto the new and seductive Westcott-Hort train which will only lead to unbelief and apostasy. Hills has rightly warned that those who take an eclectic view of providential preservation of Scriptures (ie, the Textus Receptus is good, but so is Westcott and Hort; the KJV is good, but so are all the modern versions) "are logically on [their] way toward the denial of the infallible inspiration of the Scriptures." Let me also repeat the good advice of Martin:

> The only road to progress in New Testament textual criticism is *repudiation* of their (ie, Westcott and Hort) theory and all its fruits. Most contemporary criticism is bankrupt and confused, the result of its liaison with liberal theology. A Bible-believing Christian can never be content to

follow the leadership of those who do not recognize the Bible as the verbally inspired Word of God. The Textus Receptus is the starting-point for future research, because it embodies substantially and in a convenient form the traditional text.

Gephart enjoins all his readers to be like the noble Bereans who searched the Scriptures (214). Yes, it is vitally important for all true theologues to search the Scriptures. However, it is equally important also for them to ensure that the Scriptures they search from is truly the Word of God, accurately and faithfully translated from the original. The reason is plain and simple: If you are not reading from a pure and unadulterated Word, you will not find the truth for which you seek.

Let me give an example. In the KJV, Ps 12:6–7 reads, "The words of the LORD are pure words: as silver tried in a furnace of earth, purified seven times. Thou shalt *keep them*, O LORD, thou shalt *preserve them* from this generation for ever." It is very clear from this text that God has promised to preserve His Word: He will keep and preserve "them," ie, His "words" (v6). But in the NIV, we find something quite different, "And the words of the LORD are flawless, like silver refined in a furnace of clay, purified seven times. O LORD, you will *keep us safe* and protect us from such people forever." Note the change from "keep them" and "preserve them" (KJV) to "keep us" and "protect us" (NIV). The NIV changed the pronouns from the third person plural ("them") to the first person plural ("us"). The NIV has changed the Word of God here. In the Hebrew text, the first word is תִּשְׁמְרֵם (*tishmerem*). The -em suffix is third plural, "them," not "us." He will keep "them" (so KJV) is correct. The second word is תִּצְּרֶנּוּ (*titzrennu*). The -ennu suffix is third singular with the energetic *nun*, meaning literally, "every one of them," and not "us." We therefore find Ps 12:6–7 teaching us that God will preserve His Word as a whole (plenary preservation), and His Word in its parts (verbal preservation). But the NIV by way of a "dynamic" (read "demonic") method has corrupted the text, and by so doing, removed the doctrine of Bible preservation from the Scriptures. By all means, search the Scriptures, but make sure you search from the right one!

Gephart accuses KJV-only advocates of "pride and prejudice" (215). He behaves very much like David's eldest brother—Eliab—who scolded David for wanting to fight the Philistine giant—Goliath. David wanted to defend God's name, but Eliab rebuked him saying, "I know thy pride, and the naughtiness of thine heart; for thou art come down that thou mightest see the battle" (1 Sam 17:28). This same charge is now leveled against KJV-only fundamentalists by their fellows. We reply with David, "What have I now done? Is there not a cause?" (1 Sam 17:29). Indeed, there is! There is a battle for truth to be fought today. It is against the Westcott-Hort Goliath! Are you a David, or an Eliab?

If the fundamentalists of this book—*From the Mind of God to the Mind of Man*—will not hear us, then let them hear from Dr Ian Paisley who is a friend of BJU and a prominent leader of the World Congress of Fundamentalists:

> I believe the Bible is the verbally inspired Word of the living God and because the Authorised Version is a faithful English translation of the original Hebrew of the Old Testament and the original Greek of the New Testament, it is the very Word of God in my mother tongue. Being a translation does not alter one iota of its integrity, inerrancy and infallibility as God's Word. ...

> I believe this English Authorized Version is unsurpassably pre-eminent over and above all other English translations, because like the blessed Joseph there rests upon it the blessing of the heavens above and of the deep that lieth under (Genesis 49:25).

> I cry out "There is none like that, give it me," and in so doing I nail the Satanic lie that the Authorized Version is outdated, outmoded, mistranslated, a relic of the past and only defended by stupid, unlearned, untaught obscurantists.

> As its deriders and revilers pass on to the judgment of the thrice holy God whose revelation they despise, the Old Book,

> "Incomparable in its faithfulness, majestic in its language, and inexhaustible in its spiritual fruitfulness, continues to reveal to millions the matchless grace of Him whose name is THE WORD OF GOD, and who is crowned with glory and honour."

> I believe this Book will always be the unsurpassable pre-eminent English version of the Holy Bible and no other can ever take its place.

> To seek to dislodge this Book from its rightful pre-eminent place is the act of the enemy, and what is attempted to put in its place is an intruder - an imposter - a pretender - a usurper.

We plead with BJU and fellow fundamentalists who love God and His Word to defend the KJV, and defend it only. "Shouldest thou help the ungodly, and love them that hate the LORD?" (2 Chr 19:1–2). Be like David who had the mind of God to fight Goliath. If we have the mind of God, we must also have the heart of God: "Do not I hate them, O

LORD, that hate thee? and am not I grieved with those that rise up against thee? I hate them with perfect hatred: I count them mine enemies" (Ps 139:21–22).

This paper was presented to the Fundamental Christian Ministry in its combined meeting of August 21, 2000, held at Life Bible-Presbyterian Church.

GOD'S WORD PRESERVED THROUGH THE AGES
(to the tune of Rise Up, O Men of God!)

Jack Sin

William H Walter 1825-1893

1. God's Word, In - spired and true,   Re - veal - ed to men pre - pared;
2. Pre - served by Pro - vi - dence,   The Jews - li - bra - rians were;
3. The an - cient By - zant - ine,   The text - the church re - ceived;
4. Dur - ing the Re - nais - sance,   Dawn ing - Re - form - a - tion;
5. At the Mas - ter's be - hest,   The Au - thor - ised - 's the best;
6. The Spi - rit Il - lu - mine,   Ap - ply our hearts to glean;
7. By faith we can av - er   The Bi - ble in our hands;

1. In er - rant - and in - fall - i - ble,   Its mes - sage must be read.
2. Me ti cu - lous and faith - ful,   The co - pies had en - dured.
3. Had not been - taint - ed thru the years, Of trea - sures all, most dear.
4. The Greek New - Test - a - ment ed - it,   E ras - mus, the e - lite.
5. The lang - uage - is a - bove the rest,   And passed pu - ri - ty test.
6. Each let - ter - of the Ho - ly Writ,   Di - rect - saints by its light.
7. Ac - cu rate - and re - lia - ble,   God's E - ter - nal Word will stand.

Raised up of God ...

... for such a time as this.

When seminaries and Bible colleges everywhere capitulate to the apostasy of the end time, Far Eastern Bible College stands stedfast, unmoveable, securely fastened on the Rock, even our Lord Jesus Christ, and His holy, inspired, infallible, and inerrant Word.

FEBC stands for the "old-time Gospel," the "faith which was once delivered unto the saints," in opposition to the flood of false doctrines now sweeping over the Church: Modernism, Ecumenism, Romanism, Neo-evangelicalism, Charismatism, and Postmodernism.

For sound Biblical instruction, Protestant and Reformed scholarship, come to:

Far Eastern Bible College
9A Gilstead Road, Singapore 309063
Website: http://www.febc.edu.sg
Email: febc@febc.edu.sg

Courses offered: CertRK, CertBS, DipTh, BMin, BRE, BTh, MMin, MRE, MDiv, ThM, DRE, ThD.

www.ingramcontent.com/pod-product-compliance
Lightning Source LLC
Chambersburg PA
CBHW071440090426
42737CB00011B/1731